FREEZER MEALS RECIPES

Delicious, Fast & Easy Freezer Meals for People With Busy Lives

(Quick and Easy Recipes for Busy People)

William Brown

Published by Alex Howard

© William Brown

All Rights Reserved

Freezer Meals Recipes: Delicious, Fast & Easy Freezer Meals for People With Busy Lives (Quick and Easy Recipes for Busy People)

ISBN 978-1-990169-53-3

All rights reserved. No part of this guide may be reproduced in any form without permission in writing from the publisher except in the case of brief quotations embodied in critical articles or reviews.

Legal & Disclaimer

The information contained in this book is not designed to replace or take the place of any form of medicine or professional medical advice. The information in this book has been provided for educational and entertainment purposes only.

The information contained in this book has been compiled from sources deemed reliable, and it is accurate to the best of the Author's knowledge; however, the Author cannot guarantee its accuracy and validity and cannot be held liable for any errors or omissions. Changes are periodically made to this book. You must consult your doctor or get professional medical advice before using any of the suggested remedies, techniques, or information in this book.

Table of contents

Part 1 1
Introduction 2
Main Dish Beef Freezer Recipes 7
Crock Pot Beef Stroganoff 7
Hearty Burrito Pie 9
Ziti With Meatballs 11
Crockpot Pot Roast 13
Homemade Mongolian Beef 14
Tasty Cheeseburger Casserole 16
Slow Cooked Beef With Mushrooms 18
Crock Pot Italian Beef Sandwiches 19
Sweet Potatoes And Spicy Braised Beef 20
Tex-Mex Steak Fajitas 22
Main Dish Poultry Freezer Recipes 23
Easy Chicken Enchilada 23
Chicken Enchiladas With Honey And Lime 25
Chicken Casserole With Poppy Seeds 27
Crock Pot Tex-Mex Chicken 29
Slow Cooker Orange Chicken 30
Cheese And Ham Chicken Casserole 31
Chicken Sausage And Pasta 33
Parmesan Chicken Casserole 34
Chicken Pot Pie 36
Slow Cooker Salsa Chicken 38
Slow Cooker Lemon-Lime Chicken And Rice 39

Main Dish Seafood, Vegetables And Pasta Freezer Recipes 40
Spinach Lasagna Rolls 40
Quinoa Burritos With Bean And Spinach 42
Tasty Ricotta Stuffed Shells 44
Baked Penne Pasta 46
Slow Cooker Pizza Casserole 48
Potatoes With Ham And Cheese 49
Hearty Mac And Cheese 51
Slow Cooked Tangy And Sweet Meatballs 53
Mixed Bean Enchiladas 54
Cheesy Broiled Tilapia 56
Cheesy Baked Spinach Tortellini 58
Easy Baked Spaghetti 60
Mozzarella Pasta Casserole With Tomato And Broccoli 62
Baked Penne With Spinach 64
Potato And Sausage Pockets 66
Soups Freezer Recipes 68
Yummy Black Bean Taco Soup 68
Halloween Slow Cooker Chili 69
Creamy Vegetable Chowder 71
Slow Cooked Chicken Noodle Soup 72
Slow Cooked Quinoa Chili 73
Slow-Cooker Sweet Potatoes And Vegetarian Chili 75
Farro And Chorizo Soup 77
Cannellini Bean Stew 78
Curried Chicken Soup 80

- Part 2 82
- Beef 83
- Cowboy Rice And Beans 84
- Meatballs 85
- Bierrocks 87
- French Dip Sandwiches 90
- Beef With Broccoli 92
- Ale-Marinated Steaks 94
- Beef Stroganoff 95
- Oven-Baked Barbecue Short Ribs 97
- Sweet And Sour Beef 99
- Hamburgers 102
- Garlic Beef Enchiladas 105
- Pork 108
- Pork Tenderloin In Orange Sauce 109
- Sausage Tacos 111
- Spicy Pork Chalupa 113
- Moo Shu Pork 115
- Sesame Pork 117
- Southern-Style Smothered Pork Chops 118
- Side Dishes 121
- Cooked Rice 122
- Baked Beans 123
- Garlic Bread (Like Texas Toast) 124
- Double-Stuffed Baked Potatoes 126
- Creamy Noodles 128

Mashed Potatoes	129
Freezer Cole Slaw	131
California Pilaf	133
Soups	135
Chicken Noodle Soup	136
Lentil Soup	138
Creamy Carrot Soup	140
Broccoli-Cheese Soup	142
Minestrone	144
Vegetable Chowder	147
Sausage And Bean Soup	149
Taco Soup	151
Pasta Fagioli Soup	153
White Chili	155
Sweets	157
Strawberry Granita	158
Black And White Cheesecake Squares	160
Yogurt Popsicles	162
Chocolate Pudding Cake	163
Ricotta Cheese Cookies	165
Chocolate Almond Cake	167
Miscellaneous	170
Chewy Granola Bars	171
Chicken Broth	173
Bean And Cheese Burritos	175
Stuffed Shells	176

Healthy Pancake Syrup	178
Freezing Fruit	179
Busy Bananas	181
Peanut Butter And Jelly Sandwiches	183
Homemade "Refried" Beans	185
Slow Cooker Spaghetti Sauce	187
Drop Biscuits	**Error! Bookmark not defined.**
Applesauce	**Error! Bookmark not defined.**
Pizza Kits	**Error! Bookmark not defined.**
Pizza Sauce:	**Error! Bookmark not defined.**

Part 1

Introduction

If you are a homemaker, you are responsible for providing timely and healthy meals for your household. The nutritional needs of your family cannot be effectively met if you continuously depend on delivery services. Even when you have guests, they will feel more at home when you present them with homemade meals.

For working women, balancing family and work life successfully is sometimes tricky. Many of them can be kept frozen for up to a month or longer. Instead of buying frozen items, you can make them at home and serve them along with garnishing of your choice. With this make-ahead strategy you can present your family and guests with delicious food, garnished with toppings and sauces of your choice.

The frozen meals in this collection will help you to get food ready in no time. Simply set aside some time to make the meal, freeze it and whenever it has to be served you can instantly do the job!

Many families are adopting a healthy eating lifestyle. if you want to eat healthy, you must pay attention to the ingredients that go into your food. Choosing the appropriate items to buy is sometimes a challenge. The Freezer Meals Cookbook contains the kind of recipes that are right for your family and will have them licking their fingers and asking for more!

This collection has a variety of meals to choose from, including the appropriate time required along with the details about ingredients. In addition, the ingredients used in the recipes are easily available so buying them will be no trouble. Care has also been taken to choose meals that do not require elaborate preparation.

Through this make-ahead strategy you can prepare different meals in a short amount of time and make as much as you want. You can make up to 4 or 5 recipes in a day that can be used for different days each week. Just prepare and save it for later, it is that simple!

You would not have to cook everyday with this strategy, there can be a delicious meal set on the table for your family at meal times. With this user friendly technique of just warming the frozen food after it has been thawed, even your kids can do it on their own with ease. Many types of food are well suited to freezing and they even taste better when thawed and warmed. Reheating frozen food also enables it to gain the level of warmth that was not achieved during the initial cooking so you can avoid half-cooked ingredients.

These freezer friendly recipes will compliment your cooking. Make your homemade meals easier through this hassle free process. There is a great variety from vegetable dishes to main poultry dishes. Prep, freeze and reheat the meal on whatever occasion you want.

Tips For Freezing Food

Your freezer can be one of the most important appliances in your kitchen if you use it well. Freezing keeps food within the optimum temperature that prevents the growth of food-poisoning bacteria. Your freezer can easily become a mini pantry when you freeze homemade meals and you will always have nutritious and delicious food on hand every time. To make the most of this strategy, you have to ensure that your freezer is organized properly.

Necessary Items For Freezing Homemade Food

- Plastic and foil wrap for wrapping muffins, tarts, cakes and quiches.
- Freezer paper to place between raw meat, fritters and pancake.
- Resealable freezer bags for vegetables, pancakes and fritters.
- Airtight plastic freezer-proof containers for soups, casseroles and other dishes with a lot of liquid.
- Ovenproof and freezer-proof dishes for freezing baked food.
- Labels for proper identification of frozen food.
- Permanent freezer markers for labeling (writing the name and also the use-by date on each container).

How To Store Food In the Freezer

Every item you freeze must be properly labeled with the name as well as the use-by date.

Soups And Stocks

Store in airtight containers, leaving a gap of about 1 to 1 1/2 inch at the top for the expansion of the liquid when it freezes.

Concentrated stocks And Purees

Free in ice cube trays so you can just thaw what you need at a time.

Mince

Place minced meat or vegetables in resealable plastic bag then press to flatten

Pasta bakes

Use ovenproof and freezer-proof dishes whenever you bake pasta. Let cool, cover with two layers of plastic wrap then wrap in foil before freezing.

Patties and Fritters

Arrange between sheets of freezer paper in single layers in airtight containers.

Fruits (such as berries)

Arrange on a baking tray in a single layer and freeze. Once the fruit is frozen, you can transfer to an airtight container.

Cakes, Muffins And Slices

Wrap individual slices in plastic wrap and then wrap in foil. Store together in resealable plastic bags.

Raw Meat

Wrap portions of packaged meat (steaks, chops, fillets and sausages) separately in two layers of plastic wrap before placing in an airtight container.

What You Should Not Freeze

- Vegetables that have high water content (lettuce, cucumber, celery and so on). Water expands when frozen and the structure of the cells becomes damaged. This is why they are mushy when they are thawed.
- Dairy products like cream, milk and yoghurt curdle when thawed.
- Foods with stuffing should be cooked before freezing. This is because the stuffing can absorb raw meat juices which leads to the growth of bacteria.

Refreezing Food

You can refreeze some food that you have frozen and thawed. You should however know that the refrozen food has a shorter freezer-life. It is advisable to use refrozen food within a week of putting it back in the freezer.

Refreezing cooked Food: Pasta bakes, casseroles and soups should be returned to the freezer immediately they cool down after they have been reheated. Do not refreeze food that has been left at room temperature for more than 1 or 2 hours.

Refreezing Raw Food: You can refreeze raw meat and poultry that has not been thawed for more than 48 hours in the refrigerator. Do not refreeze raw food if you have taken it out of the fridge and it has warmed up to room temperature. Discard raw food that has unpleasant odors.

Main Dish Beef Freezer Recipes

Crock Pot Beef Stroganoff

This delicious Crockpot meal takes just a few minutes to prepare but ends up with a wonderful taste.

Total time: 5-9 hours

Servings: 6

Ingredients:

3 lb stew meat

1 tsp salt

1/4 tsp black pepper

1 small yellow onion, diced

¼ tsp garlic salt

1 ½ cups of beef stock

1 tbsp ketchup

1 tbsp Worcestershire sauce

6-7 tbsp apple juice

1/3 cup flour

4-6 oz sliced mushrooms

1/2 cup light sour cream

Directions:

1. Combine stew meat, onion salt and pepper in the crock pot then stir together.

2. Combine garlic salt, beef stock, ketchup and Worcestershire sauce in a small bowl then pour over stew meat.

3. Cook on low for 7-9 hours or on high for 4-5 hours.

4. Thirty minutes to the end of the cooking time, whisk together apple juice and flour in a small bowl. Add more apple juice as needed to make a slightly thick mixture.

5. Stir flour and apple juice mixture into the crock pot, mixing well to avoid lumps. Stir in mushrooms then cook for 30 minutes on high heat.

6. Before serving, stir in ½ cup of sour cream. Serve over rice, pasta or baked potatoes.

Freezing Tip: Store in a freezer safe container. Thaw in your refrigerator for 24 hours before reheating in a saucepan over medium-low heat.

Hearty Burrito Pie

With taco meat, refried beans and vegetables, this is a tasty meal for the whole family.

Total time: 1 hour

Servings: Yields 2 8x8 casserole dishes

Ingredients:

2 lbs ground beef

2 tsp minced garlic

1 onion, chopped finely

1 (2 oz) can of black olives, sliced

1 (10 oz) can of diced tomatoes, drained

1 (4 oz) can of diced green chilies, drained

1 (16 oz) jar of red enchilada sauce (organic)

2 (16 oz) cans of refried beans (organic)

12 whole wheat flour tortillas (8 inch)

12 oz shredded cheddar cheese

Directions:

1. Preheat oven to 350°F.

2. Sauté the ground beef over medium heat in a large skillet. Add garlic and onion and sauté for another 5 minutes then drain excess fat.

3. Stir in the olives, tomatoes, green chili peppers and the enchilada sauce. Reduce to low heat and allow to simmer for about 15 to 20 minutes.

4. Meanwhile, cover one side of each tortilla with a thin layer of the refried beans then set aside.

5. Bring out 2 casserole dishes and cover the bottom of each one with a thin layer of the ground meat mixture. Cover with one prepared tortilla, followed by ground meat mixture then top with cheese. Repeat this layering until you use up the tortillas. Top everything with remaining cheese and meat mixture.

6. Bake in preheated oven for 20 to 30 minutes. Cheese should be bubbly and slightly brown.

Freezing Tip: Before baking, wrap up the casserole dishes and freeze. When to be eaten, let it sit on the counter for a few hours before baking.

Ziti With Meatballs

Total time: 1 hour

Servings: 8

Ingredients:

1 medium zucchini

1 medium onion

2 carrots

1/4 cup olive oil

Kosher salt to taste

Black pepper to taste

4 garlic cloves, chopped

1 28 oz can of whole peeled tomatoes

1 28 oz can of crushed tomatoes

1 tsp dried oregano

2 lb ground beef

2 large eggs, beaten lightly

1/3 cup bread crumbs

1/2 cup grated pecorino

1 lb ziti pasta

Green salad, for serving

Directions:

1. Fit your food processor with a coarse grating disk then grate zucchini, onion and carrots.

2. Heat oil over medium heat in a large saucepan. Add grated vegetables, 1 teaspoon salt, ½ teaspoon pepper and 1/2 of the garlic. Cook with occasional stirring for 12 to 15 minutes.

3. Add oregano, whole and crushed tomatoes with juices to the saucepan and simmer for 35 to 40 minutes. Stir occasionally, using a spoon to break up the whole tomatoes.

4. In the meantime, preheat broiler. Combine the beef with eggs, bread crumbs, remaining garlic, 1/4 cup pecorino and ½ teaspoon of salt and pepper. Using your hands, form into meatballs, (this makes 32). Arrange meatballs on a foil-lined baking sheet. Broil for 8-10 minutes, turning once.

5. Add meatballs to sauce and simmer for 5 minutes.

6. Cook pasta according to directions on package. Top with meatballs, the sauce and remaining pecorino.

Serve with salad.

Freezing Tip: Freeze the meatballs and sauce together in freezer-safe containers. They can stay for up to 3 months. When you want to reheat, place containers on counter for a few hours then transfer to a large saucepan. Cover and cook on low heat with occasional stirring until heated through. Cook pasta and serve.

Crockpot Pot Roast

This pot roast comes with a delicious mix of mouth watering sauces.

Total time: 10 hours

Servings: 6

Ingredients:

4 lb boneless chuck roast

3/4 package dry onion soup mix

3/4 cup Heinz chili sauce

12 oz Coca Cola

3/4 cup ketchup

3/4 cup dark brown sugar

2 cups baby carrots

4 new red potatoes

Directions:

1. In a crock pot, combine all the ingredients.

2. Cook for 8-10 hours on low.

Freezing Tip: Freeze before you cook or after cooking. Just put everything in a freezer bag. Even the veggies freeze well after cooking.

Homemade Mongolian Beef

Total time: 25 minutes

Servings: 4

Ingredients:

2 tsp vegetable oil

1 tbsp garlic, chopped

½ tsp minced ginger

½ cup of water

½ cup of soy sauce

¾ cup of dark brown sugar

1 lb flank steak

¼ cup of cornstarch

1 cup of olive oil , for frying

2 large green onions, chopped

Directions:

To make sauce:

1. In a medium saucepan, heat 2 teaspoon of vegetable oil over low heat. Add garlic and ginger then add water and soy sauce.

2. Pour brown sugar into the sauce, stirring until it dissolves. Increase to medium heat and let boil for 2-3 minutes. Remove from heat.

To cook the beef:

3. Slicing across the grain, cut the flank steak into 1/4-inch-thick bite-size slices. Try to make the cuts as wide as possible.

4. Dip steak pieces into cornstarch to coat both sides. Transfer to a bowl and let sit for 10 minutes.

5. Meanwhile, heat olive oil over medium heat in a large skillet. Add the beef and sauté until brown on both sides, about 2 minutes.

6. Using a slotted spoon, transfer meat onto paper towels to drain excess oil.

7. Add meat to sauce in the saucepan. Return the saucepan back to heat, add green onions then let simmer for 3-4 minutes. Serve over rice.

Freezing Tip: When cool, transfer to a freezer bag and freeze. Simply thaw and reheat when you want to eat.

Tasty Cheeseburger Casserole

Total time: 55 minutes

Servings: 12

Ingredients:

6 oz penne pasta

2 tsp of olive oil

1 onion, chopped finely

1 clove garlic, chopped finely

1 lb of lean ground beef (95% lean)

3/4 tsp salt

1/2 tsp black pepper

2 tbsp tomato paste

28 oz diced tomatoes

2 tbsp Dijon Mustard

2 cups of reduced fat cheddar cheese, grated

Directions:

1. Preheat your oven to 350°F. Prepare a 9 x 13 inch baking dish by spraying with cooking spray.

2. Cook pasta in a large pot according to directions on package. Drain.

3. Meanwhile, heat the oil in a large skillet on medium-low heat. Add onions, cook for about 5 minutes until soft then add garlic and cook for just 30 seconds.

4. Add the beef, cook until brown then season with the salt and pepper.

5. Add diced tomatoes, tomato paste and mustard. Let sauce bubble for 2 minutes until mixture thickens slightly. Season with salt and pepper if necessary.

6. Transfer cooked noodles into the prepared pan then top with meat sauce. Stir slightly, cover with foil then cook in the oven for 20 minutes. Remove from the oven, take off the foil, sprinkle cheese on top then return to oven for 5-10 minutes for the cheese to melt.

Freezing Tip: Follow steps 1 to 5 then cover properly and put in the freezer. When ready to eat, thaw and bake in oven.

Slow Cooked Beef With Mushrooms

Total time: 6-10 hours

Servings: 6

Ingredients:

3 lb stew meat, cubed

1 (10.75 oz) can cream of mushroom soup

1 oz onion soup mix

1/2 cup apple juice

2 (4 oz) can mushrooms (with the liquid)

Directions:

1. Spray a slow cooker with non-stick cooking spray, combine the ingredients in the pot and cook for 10 hours on low or 6 hours on high.

Serve over rice.

Freezing Tip: Combine the ingredients in a freezer bag and put in freezer. When you are ready to eat, thaw in refrigerator for 24 hours then follow coking directions.

Crock Pot Italian Beef Sandwiches

Besides having amazing flavor, this is also a very easy slow-cooked meal.

Total time: 12 hours

Servings: 6

Ingredients:

2 packages of dry Italian salad dressing mix

3 lb bottom round beef roast

1 16-oz jar of pepperoncini peppers

1 cup of water

Directions:

1. Add beef roast, Italian salad dressing mix and 1 cup of water to crock pot.

2. Cook for 10-12 hours on low heat.

3. When it is 2 hours to the end of the cooking time, shred the beef using two forks. Stir in the jar of pepper the continue to cook for the remaining 2 hours on low heat.

4. Serve with baked potato wedges or sandwich buns.

Freezing Tip: Freeze before you cook. Simply combine the ingredients (except water) in a freezer bag and freeze.

Sweet Potatoes And Spicy Braised Beef

Total time: 5 hours 15 minutes

Servings: 6

Ingredients:

1 1/2 lb beef chuck, cut into chunks

1 28 oz can whole peeled tomatoes

2 sweet potatoes cut into half-inch-thick semicircles

1/2 cup dried apricots

1 large red onion, cut into wedges

2 tsp ground ginger

2 tsp ground cumin

1/2 tsp cayenne

1/2 tsp ground cinnamon

Kosher salt

1 1/2 cups box couscous

1 (15 oz) can of chickpeas, rinsed

2 cups of baby spinach

1/4 cup of roasted almonds, chopped

Directions:

1. In a 6-quart slow cooker, mix together the beef, tomatoes plus juices, potatoes, apricots, onion, ginger, cumin, cayenne, cinnamon, salt and 1/2 cup of water.

2. Cover and cook for 4 to 5 hours on high or 7 to 8 hours on low.

3. Ten minutes before end of cooking time, prepare couscous according to directions on package.

4. Add chickpeas to slow cooker, cook for 2 to 3 minutes then stir in spinach.

5. Serve with couscous and sprinkle over with the almonds.

Freezing Tip: Skip the couscous and spinach. Let cooked beef cool to room temperature then transfer to freezer containers. Can be frozen for up to 3 months. When ready to eat, thaw in the fridge overnight, transfer to a pot, cover and cook for 20 to 30 minutes with constant stirring. Stir in spinach and serve with cooked couscous.

Tex-Mex Steak Fajitas

Total time: 25 minutes

Servings: 4

Ingredients:

1 lb flank steak, sliced thinly against the grain

1 jalapeno, seeded, sliced thinly

2 red bell peppers, seeded, sliced thinly

1 onion, sliced thinly

1 tsp hot sauce

1 tsp chili powder

kosher salt

4 tsp olive oil

8 (8-inch) flour tortillas, warmed

Directions:

1. In a large bowl, mix together the steak, jalapeno, red bell peppers, onion, hot sauce, chili powder and 3/4 teaspoon of salt. Make sure the steak is properly coated.

2. In a large skillet, heat 4 teaspoons of olive oil over medium heat. Add the steak, cover and cook for 10 minutes then cook uncovered for 5 minutes.

3. Serve with tortillas.

Freezing Tip: Prepare the ingredients, mix together then divide to 4. Freeze separately in 4 (1-quart) resealable freezer bags. Can be in the freezer for up to 3 months. When you want to heat, thaw then cook in hot oil in the skillet.

Main Dish Poultry Freezer Recipes

Easy Chicken Enchilada

Total time: 40 minutes

Servings: 6-8

Ingredients:

1 (10.75 oz) can of cream of chicken soup

4 chicken breasts, cooked, diced

1 (16 oz) container of sour cream

1/2 cup of milk

2 (4 oz) cans of diced green chilies

1/2 onion, diced finely

1/2 tsp garlic salt

Salt to taste

Pepper to taste

1 (10 oz) package of tortilla chips

1 cup grated cheddar cheese

1 cup grated Monterrey Jack cheese

Directions:

1. Preheat your oven to 350°F.

2. Mix all the ingredients together except the cheeses and chips.

3. Coat a 9" by 13" baking pan with cooking spray, arrange the chips in the bottom then pour the chicken mixture over the chips.

4. Sprinkle grated cheese over and bake for about 30 minutes. It should be hot and bubbly.

5. Serve with toppings of your choice.

Freezing Tip: Cook according to the directions then freeze. When you want to serve just thaw and reheat.

Chicken Enchiladas With Honey And Lime

This is a meal to make when you are expect guests in your home.

Total time: 45 minutes + 1 hour for marinating

Servings: 8

Ingredients:

For the marinade:

5 tbsp lime juice

6 tbsp honey

1/2 teaspoon garlic powder

1 tbsp chili powder

For the Enchiladas:

4 chicken breasts, cooked, shredded

8-10 flour tortillas

16 oz green enchilada sauce

1 lb Monterrey jack cheese, shredded

1 cup of heavy cream

Directions:

1. Whisk the marinade ingredients together then pour in a plastic bag. Add shredded chicken to the bag, toss then keep in refrigerator for at least 1 hour.

2. Pour 1/2 cup of enchilada sauce into a 9"x13" baking pan.

3. Transfer shredded chicken to a bowl, reserving marinade. Also reserve 1 cup of cheese for sprinkling.

4. Stuff tortillas with chicken and shredded cheese. Transfer rolled tortillas into the 9"x13" pan.

5. Mix the leftover marinade with heavy cream and remaining enchilada sauce, then pour over rolled tortillas. Sprinkle with reserved cheese.

6. Bake for 30 minutes at 350°F until crispy and brown on top.

Freezing Tip: Freeze in 3 bags before baking. The chicken, marinade and cheese in one bag, the sauce in another and tortillas in the third bag. Thaw for at least 12 hours before assembling for baking.

Chicken Casserole With Poppy Seeds

This is a delicious comfort food that is tasty and simple to make.

Total time: 45 minutes

Servings: 8

Ingredients:

2 cups of chicken, cooked, cut in 1-inch pieces

1 tbsp poppy seeds

2 cups of Ritz crackers, crushed

1 1/2 cups of sour cream

1 (10.75 oz) can of cream of chicken soup

1/2 cup of butter, melted

Directions:

1. Preheat the oven to 350°F.

2. In a large bowl, combine the chicken, chicken soup and sour cream.

3. In a second bowl, mix poppy seeds, crushed crackers and melted butter together. Stir to incorporate butter completely.

4. Spray cooking spray on a 9"x13" baking pan. Layer chicken mixture in the bottom then cover with poppy seed mixture.

5. Cover baking pan with foil then bake for 15 minutes. Remove the foil and bake for another 15 minutes.

6. Serve with cooked white rice or steamed broccoli.

Freezing Tip: Do not add the crackers if you want to freeze. You can add crackers when reheating.

Crock Pot Tex-Mex Chicken

This is an absolute winner that will be a hit with your family.

Total time: 6 hours

Servings: 6

Ingredients:

5 chicken breasts

1 (4 oz) can of diced green chilies

1 tbsp cumin

1/2 cup salsa

1/2 cup of brown sugar

1/2 can Sprite (6 oz)

Directions:

1. Mix all the ingredients together in a crock pot.

2. Cook for 5-6 hours on low heat.

3. Remove cooked chicken then shred.

4. Return chicken to crock pot then cook for 1 hour more.

5. Mix a little cornstarch with water to thicken the juices.

6. Serve with tortilla shells or black beans, tomatoes and lettuce

Freezing Tip: Once everything is cooked and chicken is shredded, transfer to a large Ziploc bag and freeze.

When you want to use, thaw for 24 hours in the fridge then reheat in the crock pot or microwave.

Slow Cooker Orange Chicken

Cooking this meal in the slow cooker makes it really easy.

Total time: 5 or 8 hours

Servings: 4

Ingredients:

4 Chicken breasts, boneless and skinless

1 cup of orange marmalade

2 tbsp soy sauce

1 cup BBQ Sauce

Directions:

1. Place chicken in the slow cooker.

2. Mix the other ingredients together then pour over the chicken.

3. Cook on low heat for 6-8 hours or high heat for 4-5 hours.

4. Shred chicken and serve over cooked white rice.

Freezing Tip: This can be frozen before you cook or after cooking.

Cheese And Ham Chicken Casserole

Total time: 55 minutes

Servings: 6

Ingredients:

3 chicken breasts, boneless and skinless, cooked and cut into 1-inch pieces

1 (6 oz) package chicken flavored stuffing mix

1 tbsp prepared, Dijon mustard

1 (10 3/4 oz) can of condensed cream of chicken soup

2 cups cooked, chopped ham

3 cups of fresh broccoli florets

6 slices of Swiss cheese

Directions:

1. Preheat your oven to 375ºF.

2. Prepare stuffing according to package directions.

3. In a medium bowl, mix the mustard and soup, add chicken, ham and broccoli.

4. Spray a 2-quart casserole dish with cooking spray then spoon the chicken mixture into it. Top with slices of Swiss cheese and stuffing.

5. Bake for 35 to 40 minutes.

Freezing Tip: Freeze before you cook or after cooking. If you cook before freezing, let it thaw completely then reheat for 20-25 minutes.

Chicken Sausage And Pasta

Total time: 40 minutes

Servings: 5

Ingredients:

1 box of farfalle pasta

12 oz of spinach chicken sausage, sliced

2-4 oz Parmesan cheese

1/2 cup of basil pesto

Directions:

1. Prepare pasta according to directions on package.

2. Mix pasta, basil pesto and cheese together in a large bowl.

3. Transfer to a baking dish, cover with foil and bake at 350°F for 20-25 minutes.

Freezing Tip: Before baking, transfer mixture to a freezer pan and freeze. You will have to bake for 40 minutes after thawing in the fridge for several hours.

Parmesan Chicken Casserole

Total time: 35 minutes

Servings: 6

Ingredients:

4 cups shredded, cooked chicken

1 jar marinara sauce

2 cups of shredded mozzarella cheese

1/2 cup of Parmesan cheese

1 cup panko

2 tbsp olive oil

Salt and pepper

Fresh, chopped basil or parsley

Directions:

1. Preheat your oven to 350°F.

2. Spray cooking on an 8x8 casserole dish.

3. Arrange chicken on the bottom of casserole dish, pour marinara sauce over then top with the cheeses.

4. In a small bowl, combine panko, fresh herbs, olive oil and a dash of salt and pepper. Mix well.

5. Sprinkle panko mixture on chicken.

6. Bake in oven for 20 to 25 minutes or until bubbling on the sides and golden on top.

Freezing Tip: Arrange everything in the casserole then freeze before you bake. When you want to cook, thaw overnight in fridge. Cover with foil before baking.

Chicken Pot Pie

Total time: 1 hour 20 minutes

Servings: 6

Ingredients:

6 chicken breasts

1 cup of frozen peas

4 medium size potatoes, peeled and cubed

2 cups carrots, sliced

1 medium onion, sliced

1 cup butter

1 cup flour

1 tsp dried thyme

2 1/2 tsp salt

1 tsp pepper

1½ cups milk

3 cups of chicken broth

1 can corn

4 pre-made pie crust

Directions:

1. In a stockpot, combine the potatoes, peas and carrot with water and boil. Once veggies are cooked, drain and set aside.

2. Meanwhile, boil chicken in another pot. When chicken is cooked, let cool, chop up then set aside.

3. Melt butter in a large skillet then sauté onion until soft. Stir in flour, thyme, salt and pepper.

4. Slowly stir in milk and broth then bring to a boil. Stir for about 2 minutes.

5. Combine the sauce with the cooked chicken, potatoes, peas and carrot. Add the corn then mix together.

6. Place 1 pie crust on the bottom of a pan. Pour half of the chicken mixture on the pie crust then cover with another pie crust. Cut 4 slits on the top of the pie crust. Repeat this layering in another pan with remaining pie crusts and chicken mixture.

7. Bake each pot pie for 35 to 40 minutes at 425ºF or until crust is browned lightly. Before cutting, let cool for 15 minutes .

Freezing Tip: Freeze before baking. Follow steps 1 to 6 then just wrap up and place in the freezer. Thaw before baking.

Slow Cooker Salsa Chicken

Total time: 4 or 7 hours

Servings: 4

Ingredients:

1 lb chicken breast

1 (10.75 oz) can cream of chicken soup

1 (16 oz) can salsa

Directions:

1. Combine ingredients in a slow cooker.

2. Cook for 3-4 hours on high or 6-7 hours on low.

3. Shred chicken then serve over a salad or in tortilla shells. You can garnish with hot sauce, lettuce, sour cream and cheese.

Freezing Tip: Freeze before cooking. Combine ingredients in freezer bag, zip the bag and freeze. Thaw in refrigerator for 24 hours before cooking.

Slow Cooker Lemon-Lime Chicken And Rice

Total time: 6 hours

Servings: 4

Ingredients:

3 lb chicken breast

12 oz lemon-lime soda (7UP)

1 (10.75 oz) can cream of chicken soup

1/4 cup of chicken broth

1 cup of white rice, raw

Directions:

1. Combine chicken, soup and 7UP in the slow cooker.

2. Cook on low for 2-3 hours.

3. Add the chicken broth and rice and cook on low for 2-3 hours more.

Freezing Tip: Freeze after cooking.

Main Dish Seafood, Vegetables And Pasta Freezer Recipes

Spinach Lasagna Rolls

If you love pasta and you are watching your weight, this is a healthy recipe that should get on your list of favorites.

Total time: 50 minutes

Servings: 9

Ingredients:

9 cooked lasagna noodles

10 oz of frozen chopped spinach, thawed and drained completely

15 oz of ricotta cheese (fat free)

1/2 cup Parmesan cheese, grated

1 egg

Salt, to taste

Pepper, to taste

32 oz jar, spaghetti sauce

9 tbsp, part skim mozzarella cheese, shredded

Directions:

1. Preheat the oven to 350°F.

2. In a medium bowl, mix together ricotta, spinach, egg, Parmesan, salt and pepper.

3. Spoon 1 cup of spaghetti sauce into a 9 x 12 baking dish.

4. Lay out lasagna noodles on a piece of wax paper. Ensure the noodles are dry then spread 1/3 cup of the ricotta mixture evenly over noodle.

5. Roll each noodle carefully then place in the baking dish with seam side down.

6. Spoon more sauce on noodles then top each with 1 tbsp of mozzarella cheese.

7. Cover the baking dish with foil then bake for 40 minutes.

8. Serve with a little sauce in a plate.

Freezing Tip: Freeze before you bake or after baking.

Quinoa Burritos With Bean And Spinach

Total time: 1 hour

Servings: 8

Ingredients:

1 1/2 cups of quinoa, rinsed

2 tbsp olive oil

1 small onion, diced

Kosher salt, to taste

Black pepper, to taste

2 tsp chili powder

2 (15.5 oz cans) of pinto beans, rinsed

3/4 cup vegetable broth (low-sodium)

2 garlic cloves, chopped

2 (10 oz) packages of frozen chopped spinach, thawed, excess liquid squeezed out

8 tortillas (10-inch)

3 cups sharp white Cheddar, grated

Sliced avocado, sour cream and salsa for serving

Directions:

1. Preheat the oven to 400° F.

2. Cook quinoa according to directions on package.

3. In the meantime, heat olive oil in a large skillet on medium heat then add onion, ½ teaspoon of salt and ¼ teaspoon of pepper. Cook with frequent stirring for 3

to 5 minutes, add chili powder and cook for 1 minute more.

4. Add broth, beans and garlic then simmer with occasional stirring for about 2 to 4 minutes or until liquid has reduced considerably. Fold in spinach.

5. Top each tortilla with about ½ cup of quinoa, ½ cup of bean mixture and 1/3 cup Cheddar. Role up tortillas to form burritos, wrap in separate pieces of heavy-duty foil then arrange on baking sheet.

6. Bake burritos for 15 to 20 minutes

7. Serve with Sliced avocado, sour cream and salsa

Freezing Tip: Place uncooked wrapped burritos in freezer bags and freeze for up to 3 months. When you want to serve, remove from the foil and heat on high in microwave until warmed through.

Tasty Ricotta Stuffed Shells

This is really simple and delicious and your family (even picky eaters) will love it.

Total time: 1 hour 15 minutes

Servings: 10

Ingredients:

1 (12 oz) package of jumbo pasta shells

2 eggs, beaten

1 lb of shredded mozzarella cheese, divided

16 oz of low-fat cottage cheese

15 oz container of low-fat ricotta cheese

8 oz of grated Parmesan cheese, divided

1 tbsp Italian Seasoning

2 tsp salt

1 tsp of ground black pepper

1 (28 oz) jar pasta sauce

8 oz of sliced fresh mushrooms

Directions:

1. Preheat the oven to 350°F.

2. Put some water in a large pot, add a little salt then bring to a boil. Add the pasta, cook for about 8-10 minutes then drain.

3. In a large bowl, combine eggs, cottage cheese, ricotta, half the Parmesan, half the mozzarella, salt, pepper and Italian Seasoning properly.

4. Stuff ricotta mixture into cooked shells then transfer to a 9x13 inch baking dish.

5. In a medium bowl, mix together the pasta sauce, reserved Parmesan and mushrooms then pour over stuffed shells. Sprinkle the reserved mozzarella cheese over everything.

6. Bake in the oven for 45 to 60 minutes or until the edges are bubbly.

Freezing Tip: Let it cool after baking then freeze. When you want to serve, just thaw and reheat.

Baked Penne Pasta

Cook this and freeze. It will be ready to eat in just a few minutes.

Total time: 55 minutes

Servings: 12

Ingredients:

1 lb dry penne pasta

1 medium onion, chopped

1 lb of lean ground beef

Garlic powder, minced garlic, pepper and onion powder to season beef

2 (26 oz) jars spaghetti sauce

8 slices of provolone cheese

1 1/2 cups of sour cream

2 tbsp grated Parmesan cheese

6 oz of mozzarella cheese, shredded

Directions:

1. Boil slightly salted water in a large pot, add penne pasta and cook for about 7-8 minutes then drain.

2. Brown ground beef and onion in a large skillet over medium heat then add spaghetti sauce, and let simmer for 15 minutes.

3. Preheat your oven to 350°F. Prepare 8x8 inch pans by spraying with non-stick cooking spray.

4. Layer in the following manner: 1/4 of penne, 1/4 of sauce, 4 slices Provolone cheese, 1/2 of the sour cream, 1/4 of penne, 1/4 of mozzarella cheese and 1/4 of the sauce mixture.

5. Top the layers with remaining mozzarella cheese and grated Parmesan cheese.

6. Cover and bake in the oven for 30 minutes.

Freezing Tip: Follow steps 1 to 5 then cover the assembled penne with 2-3 layers of foil and place in the freezer. It can last for up to 30 days in the freezer. When you want to eat, place in refrigerator for 24 hours to thaw then bake in the oven for 30 minutes.

Slow Cooker Pizza Casserole

Total time: 5 hours 20 minutes

Servings: 8

Ingredients:

1 Box uncooked Spiral Pasta

1 lb lean ground beef

1 medium onion, chopped

2 garlic cloves, minced

1 green bell pepper, diced

1/2 can olives

1 cup of pepperoni

16 oz pizza sauce

1/2 cup of water

1 cup of shredded low-fat mozzarella cheese

Directions:

1. Spray non-stick spray on the slow cooker.

2. In a medium skillet, brown the ground beef with garlic, green bell pepper and onion. Drain the excess fat.

3. Rinse the pasta and place it in slow cooker with drained ground beef mixture.

4. Stir in pepperoni and olives. Pour 1/2 cup water and the Pasta sauce over noodle mix and stir well.

5. Sprinkle shredded Mozzarella on top then cook for 4-5 hours on low heat.

6. Serve with a side of salad.

Freezing Tip: Let cool then transfer to a freezer safe container before freezing.

Potatoes With Ham And Cheese

Total time: 1 hour

Servings: 12-16

Ingredients:

1 (2 lb) package of frozen hash brown potatoes (should be thawed ahead)

½ cup of chopped onion

1 (10.75 oz) can of condensed cream of chicken soup

2 cups sour cream

2 cups of chopped ham

2 cups of Cheddar cheese (shredded)

Salt to taste

Pepper to taste

Directions:

1. Place hash browns in the refrigerator several hours before cooking time to thaw properly.

2. In a large bowl, mix together onion, chicken soup, sour cream, Cheddar cheese, salt, pepper, ham pieces and hash browns. Mix properly.

3. Transfer mixture to a 9x 13 casserole dish. Bake in preheated oven at 350°F for 45-60 minutes.

Freezing Tip: Freeze before baking. Transfer mixture to a freezer bag and freeze. Let it thaw overnight in fridge before baking.

Hearty Mac And Cheese

Total time: 1 hour

Servings: 8

Ingredients:

1 lb penne

6 tbsp unsalted butter, plus extra for the baking dishes

1/4 cup of all-purpose flour

5 cups of whole milk

Kosher salt to taste

Black pepper to taste

1 cup grated Parmesan

4 cups Cheddar, grated

1 cup of crushed buttery crackers

2 tbsp of chopped fresh parsley

Green beans, for serving

Directions:

1. Heat your oven to 350° F. Butter two 8 by 8-inch square baking dishes.

2. Cook pasta 2 minutes less than suggested on the directions on package. Drain then return to pot.

3. In a large pot, melt the butter over medium heat then add the four. Cook for 2 minutes with stirring.

4. Slowly whisk in milk, 1 teaspoon of salt and 1/4 teaspoon of pepper. Let it boil then reduce heat and

simmer with occasional stirring for 10 to 15 minutes or until the sauce becomes slightly thickened.

5. Remove from heat and stir in Parmesan and Cheddar.

6. Add the sauce to the pasta then toss together.

7. Transfer mixture to baking dishes then sprinkle with parsley and crackers.

8. Bake for 15 to 20 minute until golden. Serve with buttered green beans.

Freezing Tip: Freeze this dish unbaked. Just cover with a plastic wrap and foil. Can last up to 3 months. When you want to bake, thaw all night in the fridge. Remove the plastic wrap, cover with the foil then bake for 50 to 55 minutes. After this, uncover and bake for 5 to 10 minutes more.

Slow Cooked Tangy And Sweet Meatballs

Total time: 2 or 4 hours

Servings: 10

Ingredients:

1 (2 lb) package of frozen meatballs

1 (16-18 oz) jar of grape jelly

1 (12 oz) jar of chili sauce

Directions:

1. Combine grape jelly and chili sauce in a bowl to make a smooth mixture.

2. Mix together thoroughly with meatballs.

3. Transfer to a slow cooker and cook for 3-4 hours on low or 1-2 hours on high.

4. Serve over rice.

Freezing Tip: Before cooking, transfer the mixed ingredients into a resealable freezer bag. When you want to eat, thaw it in the refrigerator for 24 hours then cook in slow cooker.

Mixed Bean Enchiladas

Total time: 35 minutes

Servings: 8

Ingredients:

1 can red kidney beans, rinsed and drained

1 can black beans, rinsed and drained

1 can garbanzo beans, rinsed and drained

1 can cream of chicken soup

1/3 cup chopped onions

1 small can of diced green chilies

8 whole wheat tortillas

1 can enchilada sauce

1 1/2 cup shredded cheddar cheese

Directions:

1. Combine the beans, soup, chilies and onions.

2. Spoon 1/4 of this mixture into the center of each tortilla then roll up. Arrange the tortillas with seam side down.

3. Spoon the enchilada sauce over the tortillas.

4. Cover with foil and bake for 25 minutes at 350°F.

5. Remove from the oven, take off the foil, sprinkle with cheese then return to oven for the cheese to melt.

Serve topped with your choice of toppings.

Freezing Tip: Freeze before you bake. Let it thaw for a few hours before you bake.

Cheesy Broiled Tilapia

Total time: 20 minutes

Servings: 8

Ingredients:

2 lb tilapia fillets

1/4 cup real butter, softened

1/2 cup of Parmesan cheese, grated

3 tbsp Greek yogurt

Juice of 1 lemon

Zest of 1 lemon

1/4 cup of fresh basil, minced

1/4 tsp garlic powder

1/4 tsp ground black pepper

1/8 tsp celery salt

Salt and pepper

Directions:

1. Preheat broiler then grease a sheet pan with olive oil.

2. Combine butter, Parmesan, Greek yogurt, lemon juice and zest, basil, garlic powder, 1/4 tsp black pepper and celery salt. Mix well and set aside.

3. Rinse tilapia filets then pat dry. Arrange on the greased pan then season with salt and pepper on both sides.

4. Place the sheet pan a few inches from the heat and broil for 2 minutes. Flip and broil on the other side for 2 minutes.

5. Remove from the oven then spread the Parmesan topping generously on top.

6. Broil for 2 minutes more or until the top is golden and fish flakes easily.

Freezing Tip: Make the Parmesan topping, put it in a container and freeze it. Freeze fish in another container. When ready to use, thaw the fish and topping in the refrigerator overnight then follow the baking instructions.

Cheesy Baked Spinach Tortellini

This baked pasta provides a great way to make good use of leftover veggies.

Total time: 1 hour 20 minutes

Servings: Yields one 8x8 casserole

Ingredients:

1 1/2 (28 oz) jars spaghetti sauce

1/2 cup of frozen spinach, defrosted, drained and cut up

1 cup of shredded Italian mix cheese

1 cup of shredded mozzarella cheese

1 (16 oz.) package of frozen cheese tortellini, cooked al dente

Directions:

1. Preheat your oven to 375°F. Spray cooking spray on an 8x8 pan.

2. Spread a thin layer of spaghetti sauce on bottom of the baking dish. Place half of cooked tortellini over the spaghetti sauce then top with 1/2 of remaining sauce, 1/2 of spinach, 1/2 Italian cheese and 1/2 mozzarella cheese. Repeat these layers again.

3. Cover properly with aluminum foil then bake 375°F for 45 minutes.

4. Remove foil and bake for about 15 minutes more. It should be bubbly at the edges.

5. Let cool for 10 minutes before you serve.

Freezing Tip: Freeze before baking. When you are ready to bake, place in fridge to thaw overnight. Add 15 to 20 minutes to baking time.

Easy Baked Spaghetti

This comfort food is perfect for weeknight dinners, potlucks and family gatherings.

Total time: 1 hour 25 minutes

Servings: 8

Ingredients:

1 (16 oz) package spaghetti

1 lb ground beef

1 onion, chopped

1 (26 oz) jar of meatless spaghetti sauce

1/2 tsp seasoned salt

2 eggs

5 tbsp butter, melted

1/3 cup grated Parmesan cheese

4 cups of shredded mozzarella cheese

2 cups of small curd cottage cheese

Directions:

1. Cook the spaghetti according directions on package. Drain.

2. Meanwhile, add beef and onion to a large skillet over medium heat, cook until the meat is no longer pink then drain. Add seasoned salt and spaghetti sauce, stir together and set aside.

3. Whisk eggs, butter and Parmesan cheese in a large bowl. Add cooked spaghetti to the bowl and toss well.

4. Place 1/2 of spaghetti mixture into a greased 13" x 9" x 2" baking dish. Top with 1/2 of the mozzarella cheese, 1/2 of meat sauce and 1/2 of cottage cheese. Repeat layers.

5. Cover and bake for 40 minutes at 350°F. Remove cover and bake for 20-25 minutes more or until cheese melts.

Freezing Tip: Wrap up and freeze after baking. When you ready to eat, thaw and reheat.

Mozzarella Pasta Casserole With Tomato And Broccoli

Total time: 1 hour 15 minutes

Servings: 6

Ingredients:

12 oz bowtie pasta (farfalle)

1 lb frozen broccoli florets

3 large ripe tomatoes, divided

4 cloves garlic, minced very finely

3/4 lb onion, diced

3/4 cup of chopped basil leaves, divided

1 (15-oz) can of chickpeas, drained

1/2 lb fresh full-fat mozzarella, divided

3 large eggs

Juice of 1 lemon

1 cup of cottage cheese

3/4 cup of grated Parmesan, divided

2 tsp salt

1 tsp black pepper

Directions:

1. Preheat oven to 375°F. Using olive oil, grease a 9x13-inch casserole dish.

2. Cook bowtie pasta in a large pot of salted boiling water until al dente, about 11 minutes. Drain then return to pot.

3. Steam the broccoli in a stovetop steamer basket or in the microwave until just tender. Drain, chop into bite size pieces and toss with cooked pasta.

4. Cut two tomatoes into rough pieces then add to pasta. Stir in the minced garlic, onion, 1/2 cup of basil and drained chickpeas. Cut about 2/3 of the mozzarella into 1-inch chunks then stir into pasta too.

5. Whisk egg with lemon juice and cottage cheese then stir in 1/2 cup of the Parmesan. Add this mixture into the pasta and stir to combine. Stir in salt and pepper.

6. Spread pasta mixture inside the greased baking dish.

7. Cup up the remaining tomatoes into semicircles and place on top of pasta. Cut up the remaining mozzarella into tiny bits and sprinkle over tomatoes. Sprinkle the remaining Parmesan cheese on top then drizzle with olive oil.

8. Bake in the oven for 35 minutes. The casserole should bubble and cheese must be melted. Remove from oven and sprinkle the remaining basil on top.

Let stand for 10 minutes before you serve.

Freezing Tip: Freeze after cooking.

Baked Penne With Spinach

Total time: 40 minutes

Servings: 4

Ingredients:

1 tbsp olive oil

1/4 cup of oil-packed sun-dried tomatoes, chopped

2 garlic cloves, chopped

1 (15 oz) can of crushed tomatoes

1 (28 oz) can of whole tomatoes

Kosher salt & black pepper

1 tbsp balsamic vinegar

12 oz penne

1 (5-oz) package of baby spinach

2 cups of mozzarella, grated

2 tbsp Parmesan, grated

Directions:

1. Preheat the oven to 400°F.

2. In a large saucepan, heat oil then add sun-dried tomatoes and garlic. Cook for 2 minutes with constant stirring then add crushed tomatoes.

3. Using a scissors, cut up the whole tomatoes then add to saucepan. Add ½ teaspoon salt, ¼ teaspoon pepper and the vinegar. Let simmer with occasional stirring for 15 to 20 minutes, until thickened.

4. Meanwhile, add 1 tablespoon salt to water in a large pot and bring to a boil. Cook penne in the salted water for half of the time recommended in the package directions. Drain.

5. Stir spinach into the sauce, cook for about 1 minute, add the cooked pasta then toss to combine.

6. Grease an 8" x 8" baking dish. Place half of the pasta mixture in it and sprinkle with 1 cup of mozzarella. Add the remaining pasta mixture over top then sprinkle with Parmesan and the remaining cup of mozzarella.

7. Place the baking dish on a baking sheet then bake for 15 to 20 minutes until lightly browned and bubbly.

Freezing Tip: Seal unbaked pasta tightly and freeze for up to 3 months. When ready to eat, thaw and bake for 25-30 minutes.

Potato And Sausage Pockets

Total time: 1 hour 10 minutes

Servings: 6

Ingredients:

2 tbsp olive oil

6 oz of fully cooked chicken sausage links, sliced thinly

1/2 lb new potatoes, sliced thinly

1/2 lb mushrooms, sliced thinly

Kosher salt & black pepper

1 cup Cheddar, grated

1 (10 oz) package of frozen chopped spinach, thawed, squeezed dry

1 lb whole-grain pizza dough, at room temperature

A little flour, for the work surface

Directions:

1. Preheat the oven to 400°F.

2. On a rimmed baking sheet, add the oil, sausage, potatoes, mushrooms, ½ teaspoon salt, ½ teaspoon pepper and toss. Roast, for 20 to 25 minutes or until potatoes are tender, tossing once. Let cool then transfer to a bowl. Stir in the Cheddar and spinach.

3. Divide pizza dough into six pieces. On a floured surface, pull each piece of dough and roll to form a 6-inch round. Divide the spinach mixture into six portions, spoon onto one side of each round, leaving a

border of about half-inch. Fold each dough over and press the ends firmly to seal.

4. Arrange the pockets on a baking sheet lined with parchment and cut several slits on the surface of each. Bake for 20 to 25 minutes until golden brown.

Freezing Tip: Wrap up baked pockets and keep in the fridge for up to 5 days. They can be kept in the freezer for up to 3 months. When you want to eat, reheat refrigerated in the microwave for about 2 minutes and frozen for about 4 to 5 minutes.

Soups Freezer Recipes

Yummy Black Bean Taco Soup

This is a meal you can eat year-round.

Total time: 40 minutes

Servings: 6-8

Ingredients:

1 lb ground turkey

1 small onion, chopped

1 (16 oz) can of corn, undrained

1 package of mild taco seasoning mix

1 (16 oz) can of kidney beans, drained and rinsed

1 (14 oz) can of diced tomatoes

1 (14 oz) can of stewed tomatoes

1 (4 oz) can of diced green chilies

1 (8 oz) can of tomato sauce

Tortilla chips

Toppings, like sour cream or cheese

Directions:

1. Brown ground turkey and onion then drain.

2. Stir in corn, taco seasoning, kidney beans, diced tomatoes, stewed tomatoes, green chilies and tomato sauce.

3. Simmer for 20 to 30 minutes on low heat.

4. Serve with the tortilla chips and toppings that you like.

Freezing Tip: Let the soup cool after cooking then scoop into a freezer container. When it is time to eat it, thaw in fridge for about 24 hours them cook on stove or microwave until heated through.

Halloween Slow Cooker Chili

Total time: 4-8 hours

Servings: 6

Ingredients:

1 lb ground beef

1 onion, diced

1 (8 oz) can of tomato sauce

2 (14 oz) cans of diced tomatoes

1/4 cup of water

1/4 cup of ketchup

1 packet chili seasoning mix

1 (15 oz) can of dark red kidney beans

2 tbsp Worcestershire sauce

3 celery stalks, chopped

1 tbsp sugar

Directions:

1. Brown the chopped onion and beef.

2. Combine with the other ingredients in a slow cooker.

3. Stir in the browned beef and onion.

4. Cook for 6-8 hours on low or 3-4 hours on high.

5. Top with crackers and shredded cheese when serving.

Freezing Tip: Let cool then transfer into a freezer safe container.

Creamy Vegetable Chowder

This is a comforting warm bowl of soup you will appreciate on cold winter days.

Total time: 55 minutes

Servings: 8

Ingredients:

1 cup water

2 chicken bouillon cubes

1 cup of diced celery

1 cup of diced carrot

2 cups of diced potatoes

1 (10 oz) package of frozen mixed vegetables

1 can of milk

1 can cream of chicken soup

1 lb Velveeta cheese, cubed

Directions:

1. Add water, bouillon cubes, celery, carrot and potatoes to a large pot and bring to a boil. Cook until the bouillon cubes dissolve.

2. Add the frozen vegetables, reduce to low heat, cover the pot and let simmer for about 30-40 minutes. You may add water if needed.

3. Stir in the milk, cream of chicken soup and cheese. Keep stirring until the cheese melts completely. Serve with warm rolls.

Freezing Tip: When the soup has cooled down, pour it in a freezer container and freeze. When it is to be eaten, thaw in the refrigerator then microwave or reheat on the stove top.

Slow Cooked Chicken Noodle Soup

Beat the cold with this amazing soup that is also simple to make.

Total time: 7 hours

Servings: 10

Ingredients:

1 (10.75 oz) can cream of chicken soup (98% fat free)

5 cups of chicken broth

1 (15 oz) can corn, drained

1/2 small onion, chopped finely

4 large carrots, chopped finely

3 stalks of celery, chopped finely

1/2 cup of green onions, sliced

1/2 tsp garlic powder

Salt to taste

Pepper to taste

2 cans canned cooked chicken

1 1/2 cups egg noodles, uncooked

Directions:

1. Add all ingredients except the cooked chicken and noodles to the slow cooker.

2. Cook for 6 hours on low heat.

3. Add the cooked chicken and uncooked noodles, increase to high heat then cook for one hour more.

Freezing Tip: Combine everything but the chicken broth, cooked chicken and noodles in a Ziploc then freeze. Add broth to slow cooker when it is time to cook.

Slow Cooked Quinoa Chili

Total time: 5-7 hours

Servings: 12

Ingredients:

1 cup quinoa, rinsed

1 (14 oz) can of diced tomatoes with green chilies (undrained)

1 (28 oz) can of diced tomatoes (undrained)

2 (16 oz) cans of black bean, drained, rinsed

1 (15 oz) can kidney beans

1 (15 oz) can corn, drained

2 cups chicken stock

1 large size bell pepper, seeded, chopped

1 tsp garlic

1 minced onion

1 tsp cumin

1 tsp chili powder

1 tsp crushed red pepper

Directions:

1. In a 6 quart slow cooker, combine all ingredients and cook on low heat for 5-7 hours.

2. Serve warm, garnished with sour cream or cheese.

Freezing Tip: Let cool then transfer to a freezer container.

Slow-Cooker Sweet Potatoes And Vegetarian Chili

Total time: 8 hours 20 minutes

Servings: 4

Ingredients:

1 green bell pepper, chopped

1 small red onion, chopped

4 cloves garlic, chopped

1 tbsp ground cumin

1 tbsp chili powder

1/4 tsp ground cinnamon

2 tsp unsweetened cocoa powder

Kosher salt and black pepper

1 (15.5 oz) can of kidney beans, rinsed

1 (15.5 oz) can of black beans, rinsed

1 (28 oz) can of fire-roasted diced tomatoes

8 oz sweet potato (1 medium size), peeled and cut into 1-inch pieces

Tortilla chips, sour cream, sliced radishes and sliced scallions for serving

Directions:

1. In a 6-quart slow cooker, add the bell pepper, red onion, garlic, cumin, chili powder, cinnamon, cocoa

powder, 1 teaspoon of salt and ¼ teaspoon of black pepper.

2. Add the beans, tomatoes plus liquid, sweet potato and one cup of water.

3. Cover, then cook for 7 to 8 hours on low or 4 to 5 hours on high until chili has thickened and potatoes are tender.

4. Serve with tortilla chips, sour cream, sliced radishes and sliced scallions.

Freezing Tip: This chili can be kept in the fridge covered, for up to 3 days or in the freezer for up to 3 months.

Farro And Chorizo Soup

Total time: 40 minutes

Servings: 4

Ingredients:

8 oz Spanish chorizo (cured sausage), sliced

1 tbsp olive oil

1 onion, chopped

2 carrots, chopped

Kosher salt and black pepper

1 tbsp tomato paste

1/2 cup farro

4 cups chicken broth (low-sodium)

1 bunch of Swiss chard, remove stems and chop leaves roughly

1 (15 oz) can chickpeas

Directions:

1. Heat oil over medium-high heat in a Dutch oven. Brown the sausage in oil for about 2 minutes then transfer to a plate.

2. To the same Dutch oven, add onions, carrots, ¼ teaspoon each of salt and pepper. Cook with constant stirring for 4 to 5 minutes until vegetables are slightly soft.

3. Add tomato paste and stir for about 2 minutes.

4. Add farro, chicken broth and 2 cups water then bring to a boil. Turn eat down to medium and let simmer for about 15 minutes.

5. Stir in the chard, chickpeas and ½ teaspoon each of salt and pepper. Let simmer for another 3 to 5 minutes.

Freezing Tip: You can refrigerate this soup for up to 3 days or freeze for up to 3 months.

Cannellini Bean Stew

Total time: 25 minutes

Servings: 4

Ingredients:

1 (14.5 oz) can low-sodium chicken broth

2 (15 oz) cans cannellini beans, drained

6 carrots, halved lengthwise, cut into 2-inch pieces

2 garlic cloves, smashed

1 bay leaf

3 cups of fresh spinach leaves

Kosher salt and black pepper

2 tbsp extra-virgin olive oil

Directions:

1. In a Dutch oven, combine the broth, beans, carrots, garlic and bay leaf then bring to a boil over medium heat.

2. Cover, turn down heat and let simmer for about 15 minutes until carrots are tender. Remove the bay leaf and discard.

3. Add ½ teaspoon of salt, ¼ teaspoon of pepper and the spinach and stir for 1 minute. Serve warm.

Freezing Tip: You can refrigerate for up to 3 days or freeze for up to 3 months.

Curried Chicken Soup

Total time: 1 hour

Servings: 8 (2 cups each)

Ingredients:

2 tbsp canola oil

1 cup of diced carrots

1 large sweet onion, diced

1 cup of diced celery

2 cloves of garlic, minced

6 cups of chicken broth

1 lb sweet potatoes, peeled, cubed

1 lb Yukon gold potatoes, peeled, cubed

3 cups of fresh yellow corn kernels

4 cups of shredded cooked chicken

2 cups of uncooked, shelled frozen edamame

1 (13.5 oz) can of unsweetened coconut milk

2 tsp table salt

1 tsp ground black pepper

1 tbsp curry powder

Toppings: peanuts, toasted coconut, green onions, lime wedges

Directions:

1. Heat oil in a stockpot and sauté carrots, onions and celery over medium-high heat for 5 minutes. Add garlic and cook for 1 minute.

2. Add chicken broth and the remaining ingredients then bring to a boil with frequent stirring.

3. Reduce to medium heat and let simmer for 20 to 25 minutes, stirring occasionally.

Serve with preferred toppings.

Freezing Tip: Let cool completely then transfer to a freezer bag. Freeze up to one month. Thaw in fridge for 8 hours before reheating.

Part 2

Beef

While hamburger is the most freezer-friendly meat, don't forget about steak, roasts and beef dishes that can be frozen. There are a wide array of beef dishes that can be frozen in an entirely cooked state or that can be frozen in components.

Cowboy Rice And Beans

Serves 8 (you can freeze in 2 bags of 4 servings each).
Method: Prepare recipe and freeze, and then reheat when ready to eat.

Ingredients:
- 1 pound lean ground beef (85% lean or leaner)
- ½ onion, chopped
- ¾ c. water
- ¾ teas. chili powder
- ½ teas. salt
- 1 (15 oz.) can pinto beans, drained and rinsed
- 1 (4 oz.) can chopped green chilies, undrained
- 1 c. long-grain rice, uncooked

To prepare for the freezer: Cook meat and onion in a large skillet until the meat is brown and cooked through. Drain the meat in a colander and rinse with fresh water; drain off the water. Pat dry with paper towels.

Combine the meat and the rest of the ingredients except for the rice. Place this mixture in a large freezer bag. Put the rice in a smaller freezer bag. Put all bags together in a large freezer bag and freeze.

When you're ready to eat: Thaw overnight in refrigerator. Mix rice into other ingredients and place everything into a 3-quart baking dish sprayed with non-stick spray. Cover dish and bake at 350 degrees for 50 minutes. Stir; cover and bake an additional 30 minutes or until the rice is tender and cooked through.

Meatballs

These meatballs are made heartier by the addition of rice. This makes your meat go further and adds a nice element to what is otherwise a basic staple item in your freezer. Double or triple the recipe to make enough for several meals.

Serves 4.
Method: Cook the meatballs and heat on the day you want to eat them.

Ingredients:
- 1 lb. ground beef (85% lean or leaner)
- 3 slices whole wheat bread
- 1 egg, beaten
- 1 c. milk
- ½ c. onion, chopped fine
- 1 rib celery, chopped fine
- ¼ c. carrots, chopped fine

- ¼ c. uncooked rice
- 1 teas. salt
- 3 cups V-8 juice

To prepare for the freezer: Place crumbled bread into a bowl with the milk. Add the beaten egg to this mixture. Let sit for 15 minutes or so.

Meanwhile, mix remaining ingredients, using your clean hands to get everything well mixed. Add the bread/milk mixture to the meat mixture and mix well. Shape into 2 ½-inch meatballs; using a cookie baller can make this much easier. Place the meatballs in a single layer in a baking pan and pour the juice over. Bake at 350 for 30 to 45 minutes, or until the meatballs are cooked thoroughly. Freeze the meatballs in the juice in a freezer bag or foil pan.

When you're ready to eat: Thaw overnight in the refrigerator. Bake at 350 degrees until hot or microwave until hot.

Bierrocks

Method: Cook completely and freeze. Simply heat and eat.

Makes about 15 bierrocks.

Ingredients:

- 2 cups 1% milk, at room temperature
- 2 packages yeast
- ¼ c. vegetable oil
- 2 eggs, beaten
- 1 teas. salt
- 6 c. all-purpose flour
- 1 ½ to 2 lb. ground beef
- ½ head cabbage, chopped fine

- 1 large onion, chopped

- 15 slices American or Monterey Jack cheese

To prepare for the freezer: Mix the milk and oil together in a bowl. Add eggs, yeast, sugar, salt and about 5 cups of the flour. Mix well and add remaining flour if needed to form a kneadable dough. Knead for a few minutes; cover bowl and let the dough rise in a warm place for about an hour or until doubled.

Meanwhile, brown the ground beef in a large skillet until cooked. Add onion and cabbage and continue cooking until the onion is soft and the cabbage is wilted. Add the salt, pepper, and other seasonings you might like (such as onion powder or garlic powder) to taste. Let cool.

When dough is ready, roll out hunks that are the size of tennis balls to thin discs; try to get them as thin as possible. Place a half piece of cheese on the dough, top with hamburger filling and top with the other half slice of cheese. Fold over like a turnover and seal well.

Place the turnovers on a baking sheet and brush with beaten egg if you like. You can also sprinkle with sesame seeds if you want. Bake at 350 degrees for about 30 minutes or until golden.
Cool and place into freezer bags.

When you're ready to eat: Take straight from the freezer and place in a 325 degree oven. Cook until hot, about 30 minutes.

French Dip Sandwiches

If you are fan of cheesy hot sandwiches that are served with an au jus, you are in luck. This flavorful recipe is easy to make in your slow cooker and will provide a warming meal at the end of a long day.

Serves 4.
Method: Cook and shred meat, then thaw and heat when you're ready to eat.

Ingredients:

- 4 lb. beef chuck roast
- ½ c. red wine or low-sodium chicken broth
- 1 clove garlic, minced
- 1 tab. fresh rosemary (or 1 ½ teas. dried)
- 12 whole black peppercorns
- ¼ c. low-sodium soy sauce
- 3 beef bouillon cubes
- 1 bay leaf

To have on serving day:
- 4 slices of cheese (provolone works well)
- Good quality buns

To prepare for the freezer: Combine the meat in a slow cooker with the wine or chicken broth, garlic, rosemary, pepper, soy sauce, beef bouillon and bay leaf. Add 4 cups of water and cook on high for 1 hour, then lower heat to low for 8 to 10 hours.

When the meat is done, remove from the slow cooker and shred it with 2 forks. Season the liquid in the slow cooker with salt and pepper to taste. Place the meat in one freezer bag and the liquid in another or put the liquid in a plastic container.

When you're ready to eat: Thaw bags overnight in the refrigerator. Preheat oven to 350 degrees. Heat meat in microwave while you reheat liquid in a small saucepan on the stove. Place meat on one side of each bun and add cheese. Place top of bun on sandwich, place sandwiches on a baking sheet and bake for about 6 to 8 minutes, or until the cheese is melted and the bun is crunchy. Serve the liquid on the side for dipping.

Note: You can also freeze the uncooked meat with the other ingredients and cook on your serving day, following the same instructions.

Beef With Broccoli

This popular Chinese restaurant favorite is a cinch to make at home. Prep ahead and keep the beef in the freezer. Getting this on the table is fast and easy.

Serves 4.
Method: Freeze meat in the marinade; cook fresh on serving day.

Ingredients:
- 1 pound lean boneless beef (such as sirloin)
- ¾ c. low-sodium beef broth
- 1/3 c. low-sodium teriyaki sauce
- 2 teas. cornstarch
- ¼ teas. dried crushed red pepper
- 2 cloves garlic, minced

To have on serving day:
- 1 teas. vegetable oil
- 4 c. fresh broccoli florets
- 1 medium-sized red pepper, seeded and cut into thin strips
- 4 c. cooked long-grain white rice or brown rice

To prepare for the freezer: Trim the fat from the steak and slice into thin strips. Place the meat into a freezer bag and add the marinade ingredients (from beef broth to garlic). Mix well and place bag in the freezer.

When you're ready to eat: Thaw meat overnight in the refrigerator. Drain the meat and reserve the marinade, putting it into a small saucepan. Bring the marinade to a boil and cook for 1 minute. Remove from heat and set aside.

Meanwhile, heat oil in a large skillet or wok. Add meat and stir fry for about 5 minutes or until cooked. Remove meat from the skillet and set aside. Add the broccoli and pepper to the skillet. Stir fry the vegetables for 3 minutes. Add the meat and reserved marinade to the skillet. Stir fry for about 2 minutes or until thickened. Serve over rice.

Ale-Marinated Steaks

These steaks are tender, delicious and a cinch to make since you freeze them in the marinade and they have plenty of time to get tender and juicy. This recipe is great for a special occasion meal; keep these on hand at all times so you can make a special meal anytime.

Serves 4.
Method: Freeze steaks in marinade and grill or broil when ready to eat.

Ingredients:

- 4 New York steaks (about 8-10 ounces each)
- 2 tab. chopped fresh cilantro
- 4 cloves garlic, minced
- 1 teas. salt
- 1 teas. pepper
- 1 teas. crushed red pepper flakes
- 1 bottle ale
- ¼ c. olive oil

To prepare for the freezer: Combine all marinade ingredients in a small bowl; stir well. Pour this mixture into a freezer bag. Add steaks, seal and freeze.

When you're ready to eat: Let thaw overnight in the refrigerator. Remove the steaks from the marinade and grill or broil 5 minutes per side for rare to medium rare. Serve immediately (and with a pat of butter if desired).

Beef Stroganoff

Serves 4.
Method: Partially cook and finish on the day you're going to eat.

Ingredients:
- 1 ½ pounds beef, such as boneless sirloin or round steak, cut into thin strips
- ¼ c. butter
- 1 large onion, chopped fine
- 1 clove garlic, minced
- 2 c. mushrooms, sliced
- 1/3 c. dry white wine OR 1/3 c. low-sodium chicken broth
- Salt
- Pepper

To have on serving day:
- 1 ¼ c. sour cream

- Cooked egg noodles

To prepare for the freezer: Melt 2 tablespoons butter in a large skillet and brown the steak strips. Remove and set aside. Add the remaining 2 tablespoons butter and add onions and garlic, cooking until both are soft but not brown. Add the mushrooms, the wine or broth, salt and pepper. Simmer for about 5 minutes.

Put the meat into a freezer bag and add the sauce. Let cool and freeze.

When you're ready to eat: Thaw overnight in the refrigerator. Pour contents of bag into a large skillet and heat for about 20 minutes, or until the beef is thoroughly cooked. Stir in sour cream just before serving. Serve over egg noodles.

Oven-Baked Barbecue Short Ribs

Serves 4
Method: Freeze uncooked ribs in marinade to cook later.

Ingredients:

- 1 c. vinegar
- ½ c. Ketchup
- ½ c. honey
- ½ onion, chopped
- 3 tab. Worcestershire sauce
- ½ teas. salt
- ½ teas. mustard
- ½ teas. paprika
- 1 teas. garlic powder
- ½ teas. pepper
- 3-4 pounds beef short ribs on the bone

To prepare for the freezer: In a small saucepan combine all ingredients except ribs. Bring to a boil, cover and reduce heat to low. Cook for 10 to 15 minutes. Put 1 cup of the marinade on a small plastic container and set aside. Let the remaining marinade cool. Place ribs in a large freezer bag and pour marinade over the ribs. Seal. Label bag and plastic container and place in freezer.

When you're ready to eat: Thaw ribs and sauce overnight in the refrigerator. Put ribs in a roasting pan and pour sauce from the bag over the ribs. Cook at 325 for 1 to 2 hours or until tender. Baste frequently with the extra sauce.

Sweet And Sour Beef

Serves 4-6.

Method: Brown meat and freeze with other recipe components, and then cook in slow cooker when ready to eat.

Ingredients:

- 1 ½ lb. beef, cut into 1" pieces
- 1/3 c. packed brown sugar
- 1/3 c. cider vinegar
- 1 small can of pineapple chunks (reserve juice)
- 3 tab. soy sauce
- 1 clove garlic, minced
- 3 tab. oil

- ½ teas. dried red pepper flakes

To have on serving day:

- 3 c. baby carrots, cut into strips
- 1 large green pepper, cut into chunks
- 1 large onion, cut into quarters and separated
- 3 tab. cornstarch
- 3 tab. water
- Cooked rice

To prepare for the freezer: Combine the sugar, vinegar, pineapple juice, soy sauce and minced garlic in a bowl. Add the brown sugar, stirring until the sugar dissolves completely. Pour into a small freezer bag. Put pineapple in another small freezer bag.

Season the beef with salt and pepper to taste. Heat the oil in a large skillet and brown the beef with the red pepper flakes until brown. Cool and put meat into a freezer bag. Place all the freezer bags into a gallon-sized freezer bag and freeze.

When you're ready to eat: Thaw meat, sauce, and pineapple overnight in refrigerator. Place all into a slow cooker and add onion and carrots. Reserve green pepper for later use. Cook on high for 3-4 hours or on low for 7-8 hours or until meat is cooked.

When cooked, turn slow cooker to a high setting (if not already on high) and whisk cornstarch and water together in a small bowl. Add the mixture and the green pepper to the slow cooker and cook about 30 minutes or until sauce is thickened. Serve over cooked rice.

Hamburgers

Keep hamburger patties on hand in the freezer for quick hamburger meals anytime. It might seem like a simple thing – and it is – but when you want to cook burgers, you'll be thrilled with how easy it is to put them together when you have formed and ready hamburgers in the freezer.

Serves varied amount depending on how many you make.

Method: Season hamburger, form into patties and freeze.

Basic hamburgers

Ingredients:

- Hamburger
- To have on serving day:
- Salt
- Pepper
- Fixings for hamburgers

To prepare for the freezer: Form hamburger into patties, flattening them so they are about ½-inch thick. Wrap each hamburger patty in plastic wrap and store them in a freezer bag.

When you're ready to eat: Thaw hamburger patties on countertop until ready to cook, about 2 hours. (Don't let the meat get to room temperature; it should still be cold.) Season each side with salt and pepper and cook, flipping evenly, until done.

Tex-Mex Hamburgers

Ingredients:

- Hamburger
- Hot red pepper sauce

To have on serving day:

- Salt
- Pepper
- Fixings for hamburgers
- Salsa (optional)
- Guacamole (optional)

To prepare for the freezer: Put hamburger into a bowl and mix in hot pepper sauce, about 1 teaspoon (or to taste) per 1 ¼ pound of hamburger. Form hamburger into patties, flattening them so they are about ½-inch thick. Wrap each hamburger patty in plastic wrap and store them in a freezer bag.

When you're ready to eat: Thaw hamburger patties on countertop until ready to cook, about 2 hours. (Don't let the meat get to room temperature; it should still be cold.) Season each side with salt and pepper and cook, flipping evenly, until cooked.

Garlic Beef Enchiladas

This recipe is more of a casserole type of dish, but even if you are not fond of casseroles or enchiladas, give this one a try. It's a delicious tried-and-true favorite.

Serves 8 (divide into 2 foil pans to make 2 dinners for 4 people each).
Method: Make these and freeze; bake when ready to eat.

Ingredients:

Enchiladas:

- 1 to 1 ½ lb. ground beef
- 1 small onion, chopped
- 2 tab. all-purpose flour
- 1 tab. chile powder
- 1 teas. salt
- 2 cloves garlic, minced
- ½ to 1 teas. cumin
- ¼ teas. sage
- 1 can (14 ½ oz.) stewed tomatoes

Sauce:

- 5 cloves garlic, minced
- ¼ c. unsalted butter
- ½ c. flour
- 1 (14 ½ oz.) can low-sodium beef broth
- 1 (15 oz.) can tomato sauce
- 1 ½ tab. chile powder
- 1 ½ teas. ground cumin
- 1 ½ teas. sage
- ¼ to ½ teas. salt
- 10 (7-inch) flour tortillas
- 1 c. shredded co-jack cheese

To have on serving day:

- 1 cups shredded co-jack cheese (1/2 c. for each casserole)

To prepare for the freezer: In a large skillet set over medium heat, cook the beef and onion until the onion is tender and the meat is no longer pink. Drain meat and add back to pan. Add flour and seasonings. Mix well and add tomatoes. Bring to a boil. Reduce the heat, cover, and simmer for 15 minutes.

Meanwhile, in a medium saucepan set over medium heat, sauté the garlic in the butter until soft, but not brown. Stir in the flour until well blended. Slowly stir in the beef broth, and then bring to a boil. Cook and stir the mixture for 2 minutes or until it's bubbly. Stir in the tomato sauce and the seasonings. Stir until everything is heated through.

Pour ¾ c. sauce into each of 2 9" x 9" foil baking pans (or pour 1 ½ c. in a 13" x 9" if making just one casserole). Spread a small amount of beef mixture in each tortilla (about ¼ c.) and top with about 2 tablespoons of cheese. Roll each up tightly and place, seam side down, in the pan. Top all the enchiladas with the remaining sauce. Wrap well and freeze.

When you're ready to eat: You can cook these from frozen or cook them after you have defrosted them.

To cook from frozen, place baking pan or dish in a 350-degree oven and cook covered for 50 minutes to 1 hour or until hot and cooked through. Remove from the oven and sprinkle with about ½ c. of co-jack cheese. Bake, uncovered for another 10 minutes or until the cheese is melted.

To cook from a thawed state, bake for 30 minutes, then uncover and add cheese, following instructions above.

Pork

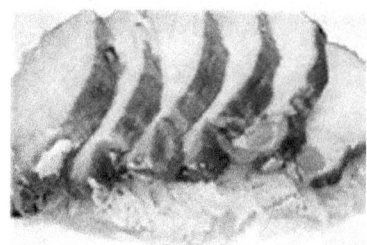

When planning a freezer session, don't forget pork. It freezes well, is versatile and inexpensive. Examine your favorite pork dishes and then apply what you know about freezer cooking to make them freezer-friendly.

Pork Tenderloin In Orange Sauce

If you like the combination of orange and pork, you'll enjoy this dish.

Serves 4.
Method: Freeze the pork tenderloin in the marinade and cook when ready to eat.

Ingredients:

- ¾ c. orange juice
- 1/3 c. low-sodium soy sauce
- 4 teas. minced garlic (about 4 cloves)
- 2 whole pork tenderloins (about 1 ½ pounds total)
- Salt and pepper to taste.

To prepare for the freezer: Place tenderloins in a freezer bag. Mix marinade ingredients (except salt and pepper) and pour over the tenderloins. Place in freezer.

When you're ready to eat: Thaw tenderloins overnight in the refrigerator. Preheat oven to 400 degrees. Remove the pork from the marinade and place on a baking sheet. Bake until done to 160 degrees, about 20-30 minutes. While the pork is cooking, pour marinade into a small saucepan and cook for 2-4 minutes at a simmer. Slice pork when cooked and pour sauce over it.

Sausage Tacos

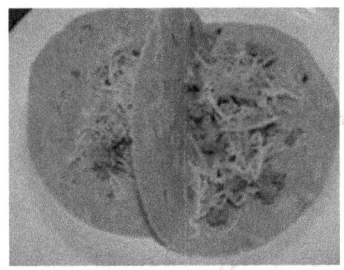

This might sound like an unusual recipe, but it's delicious and freezes very well. Play around with the cheeses because you might like something a bit spicier or something milder. Because you are starting with hot sausage, consider that carefully when choosing your cheese. This is one of the simplest of all freezer recipes and heats quickly for a super-fast meal.

Serves 4.
Method: Cook and freeze. Reheat when ready to eat.

Ingredients:
- 1 pound spicy Italian pork sausage
- ½ white onion, chopped fine
- Red pepper flakes (optional)

To have on serving day:
- Colby-jack cheese, shredded

- Store-bought handmade corn tortillas
- Lettuce, onion, tomato

To prepare for the freezer: Brown the sausage for about 5 minutes and then add onion. Break up the sausage with a spoon and continue cooking until the sausage is cooked and the onion is translucent. If you like things spicier, add a dash of hot pepper flakes. Place cooked sausage into a freezer bag and freeze.

When you're ready to eat: Thaw overnight in the refrigerator. Place contents of into a baking pan sprayed with non-stick spray; sprinkle with cheese and bake at 350 for about 20 minutes or until heated through and the cheese is melted. Serve on handmade corn tortillas with lettuce, onion and tomato, if desired.

Spicy Pork Chalupa

This dish makes generous portions, is inexpensive, relatively healthy and freezes well for a speedy meal anytime you need it. Make this on your cooking day and enjoy for dinner that night, freezing the leftovers.

Serves 8 to 10 (freeze in as many bags as you think works for your family).
Method: Cook and freeze, reheating when ready to eat.

Ingredients:

- 1 lb. dry pinto beans
- 1 pork loin roast (about 3-4 pounds), trimmed
- 7 c. water
- ½ onion, diced fine
- 3 cloves garlic, minced
- 3 tab. chili powder
- 1 tab. salt
- 1 teas. oregano
- 1 (4 oz.) can chopped green chilies

To have on serving day:

- Cheddar cheese

- Salsa

- Tortillas

To prepare for the freezer: Rinse pinto beans. Place all ingredients into a large stock pot. (You don't need to soak the beans for this, just make sure they are rinsed well.) Bring the contents of the pot to a boil and reduce heat, cover, and simmer until beans and pork are tender. Add more water if necessary. Cooking time depends on the roast, but total cook time is generally somewhere between 4 and 6 hours. Remove the roast, let cool slightly, and then shred the meat. Return the meat to the pot and simmer until the mixture is thickened, about 30 minutes.

Freeze pork and beans in freezer bags.

When you're ready to eat: Thaw overnight in refrigerator. Reheat in microwave or oven until hot. Serve with tortillas, cheese and salsa.

Moo Shu Pork

A little pork goes a long way in this dish, making it an affordable meal. This dish requires some cooking on the serving day, but your meat will already be cooked, so you only need to finish the dish off. It's worth the little bit of extra work.

Serves 4.
Method: Partially cook and finish before eating.

Ingredients:
- 1 (about 1 ½ lb.) pork tenderloin, sliced into 2" x ¼" strips
- 1 tab. low-sodium soy sauce
- 2 cloves garlic, minced
- 2 teas. canola oil

To have on serving day:
- 1 teas. canola oil
- 1 tab. low-sodium soy sauce
- 1 tab. hoisin sauce
- 2 c. shredded Napa cabbage
- 1 c. mushrooms, sliced
- 1 med. Sweet red pepper, seeded and cut into thin strips

- 1 c. bean sprouts
- ¼ c. plum sauce
- 8 (7-inch) flour tortillas

To prepare for the freezer: Heat a large skillet or wok over medium-high heat; add oil. Mix the pork, 1 tablespoon soy sauce and garlic. When hot, add the pork in its marinade and cook, until browned.

Place the pork into a freezer bag and place in freezer.

When you're ready to eat: Thaw pork overnight in the refrigerator. Place a work or large skillet over medium-high heat and add oil and wait until hot. When hot, add the cabbage, mushrooms and the pepper; stir fry for 2 minutes. Add the bean sprouts and cook for 2 minutes. Add the pork to the wok or skillet along with 1 tablespoon of soy sauce and the hoisin sauce. Stir fry 2 minutes or until thickened.

Meanwhile, heat tortillas in the oven or microwave until hot.

To serve, spoon a small amount of plum sauce (about 1 ½ teaspoons) over one side of each tortilla; top with pork mixture. Roll up the tortillas and serve immediately.

Sesame Pork

Serves 6.

Method: Cook about halfway through and complete cooking on the day you're going to eat these pork chops.

Ingredients:
- ¼ teas. salt
- ¼ teas. pepper
- 6 center-cut pork chops (about ¾ to 1-inch thick each)
- 2 teas. sesame oil
- ¾ c. chicken broth (low sodium preferred)
- 3 tab. sesame seeds, toasted
- 1 tab. brown sugar
- 2 tab. red wine or cider vinegar
- 1 tab. Dijon mustard

To prepare for the freezer: Sprinkle the salt and pepper over both sides of the pork. Heat oil in a large nonstick skillet over medium heat. When hot, add the pork chops and cook for about 3 minutes on each side or until brown. Add the broth, sesame seeds, brown sugar, vinegar and mustard. Cover and reduce heat, simmering for 20 minutes. Let cool and place sauce and pork chops into a freezer bag or foil pan. Freeze.

When you're ready to eat: Thaw chops overnight in the refrigerator. Place chops in a baking dish and spread sauce all over. Bake in 350-degree oven for about 20 to 30 minutes or until heated through. Serve sauce over pork.

Southern-Style Smothered Pork Chops

These flavorful and savory pork chops will make your kitchen smell wonderful; the taste will match that smell! There are a number of steps required to get these chops in the freezer, but you get two meals out of it, so it's worth the work.

Makes 8 total servings.
Method: Cook until nearly done and then freeze to finish cooking before eating.

Ingredients:
- 4 slices bacon, cut into 1-inch pieces
- 4 tablespoons flour
- 2 cans (14 ½ oz. each) chicken broth
- Vegetable oil
- 8 bone-in pork chops, about 1/2-inch thick
- Ground black pepper

- 2 medium yellow onions, sliced thin
- Salt
- 4 teaspoons minced garlic
- 2 teaspoons dried thyme

To have on serving day:
- Bay leaf

To prepare for the freezer: Fry bacon in a small saucepan over medium heat; cook until lightly browned, about 10 minutes. Using a slotted spoon or spatula, remove the bacon from the pan and leave drippings behind. You need 4 tablespoons of fat; if you have too much, remove some and if you need more, supplement with vegetable oil.

Reduce heat to medium-low and whisk the flour into the fat until the mixture is smooth and creamy. Cook, whisking constantly, until the mixture is light brown, about 3-5 minutes. Whisk the chicken broth in slowly; increase the heat and bring to a boil, stirring only occasionally. Cover the pan and set it aside off the heat.

In a 12-inch skillet set over high heat, heat 1 tablespoon of oil. While waiting for the oil, dry all of the pork chops with a paper towel and sprinkle with ground black pepper. When the oil is smoking (about 3 minutes) add 4 pork chops to pan and brown until they are a deep golden brown. Flip the chops and cook until they are browned on the second side, about 3 minutes.

Transfer the chops to a plate and repeat process with the second batch of 4 chops.

In each of two gallon-sized freezer bags, place 4 of the browned pork chops.

To the pan that you cooked the pork chops in, add 2 tablespoons of oil, the onions and ½ teaspoon of salt. Using a wooden spoon, scrape the browned bits from the bottom of the skillet and cook the onions until they are brown around the edges and softened, about 5-7 minutes. Stir in the garlic, and cook 2 minutes. Add thyme and cook until the mixture is fragrant, about 30 seconds more.

Divide the sauce evenly among the 2 bags with the pork chops. Let cool and when cool, freeze.

Side Dishes

There are many side dishes that can be made ahead. Imagine the convenience of pulling not just a dinner entrée out of the freezer, but a side dish or two as well.

Cooked Rice

At first blush, this might not seem like a freezer dish; nor does it seem like an exciting thing to make and put up in the freezer. It's just rice. But if you think about how much time you can save when you have rice made and ready to eat, you can easily see how adding it to your freezer session is critical. Make several bags and keep them on hand at all times. You can freeze cooked brown or white rice, but we'll use white rice in this recipe.

Serves 4.
Method: Cook rice and freeze in bags. Reheat when it's time to eat.

Ingredients:
- 1 cup white rice
- 2 cups water

To prepare for the freezer: Bring water and rice to a boil in a medium saucepan. Once it is boiling, lower heat and cook until done, about 20 minutes. Let cool. Once cool, place in quart-sized freezer bags and freeze.

When you're ready to eat: There's no need to thaw. Open the bag and place in the microwave, heating in 1 minute intervals until hot.

Baked Beans

Serves 4.
Method: Mix all ingredients and reheat when ready to eat.

Ingredients:
- 1 small onion, chopped
- 1 teas. olive oil
- ½ c. packed brown sugar
- 1 tab. molasses
- 2 tab. Worcestershire sauce
- 2 (16 oz.) cans kidney beans, drained and rinsed
- 1 (16 oz.) can white beans, drained and rinsed

To prepare for the freezer: Sauté onion in olive oil until cooked (about 5 minutes). Add all remaining ingredients and cook for a few minutes or until everything is mixed well and flavors are melded. Add salt and pepper to taste. Cool to room temperature and freeze in a large freezer bag.

When you're ready to eat: Let thaw overnight in refrigerator and pour contents of bag into a small saucepot. Cook until heated through.

Garlic Bread (Like Texas Toast)

This is so much better than the frozen garlic bread (Texas toast) you can buy in the freezer section of the grocery store. Make a big batch of this and enjoy it with pasta dishes, chicken dishes, whenever you like. Best of all, you know what's in it and you can control the fat by reducing the butter.

Makes 24 slices of garlic bread.
Method: Make and freeze; heat and crisp up when ready to eat.

Ingredients:
- 2 ½ sticks butter
- 8 finely minced cloves garlic
- ½ teas. sugar
- ½ teas. salt
- ½ teas. pepper
- 24 (1-inch) slices of French or Italian bread

To prepare for the freezer: Beat butter, garlic, sugar, salt and pepper in a bowl with a fork until well combined. Spread the butter mixture evenly over both sides of bread.

Line a large baking sheet with waxed paper and lay the slices of bread on the sheet and freeze until firm, about 15 to 30 minutes. Once firm, transfer the bread slices to a gallon-sized freezer bag and freeze for up to 2 months.

When you're ready to eat: Preheat oven to 425 degrees. Pull out only as many pieces of bread you need and lay them on a rimmed baking sheet. Bake for about 10 minutes or until golden brown on one side. Flip them over and bake until golden on the second side, about 5 to 7 minutes more.

Double-Stuffed Baked Potatoes

These are great alongside a steak or chicken dish. Or make a big green salad and enjoy these as a side to your big salad dinner. Leave the bacon out to keep these vegetarian.

This recipe makes 20 baked potato halves.
Method: Cook and freeze, reheating when ready to eat.

Ingredients:
- 10 russet potatoes
- 6 strips of bacon
- ½ teas. onion powder
- 4 tab. unsalted butter, melted
- 4 ounces of sour cream
- 2 ounces grated cheddar cheese

- ½ teas. each salt and pepper

To prepare for the freezer: Scrub potatoes and place on a baking sheet. Poke all over with a fork. Bake at 400 for about an hour or until tender (length of cooking will depend on the size of the potato). Once tender, remove from oven and let cool.

Meanwhile, cook bacon in pan until tender-crisp. Drain on paper towels and let cool. Melt butter.

Carefully, slice the potatoes in half lengthwise and scoop out the potato, leaving a shell of the skin. Put the potato in a bowl and add bacon you've crumbled, the onion powder, the butter, the sour cream, cheddar cheese and salt and pepper. Mix well.

Spoon this mixture back into the potato shells, being careful not to break the shells. Place these on a baking sheet lined with waxed paper. Place into freezer and freeze until hard. Once hard, place into freezer bags. Freeze.

When you're ready to eat: Pull out the number of potatoes you want to cook and place into a 350 degree oven for about 30 to 45 minutes or until heated through. These can also be heated in the microwave for about 5 minutes total (check every few minutes and remove them from the oven when hot).

Creamy Noodles

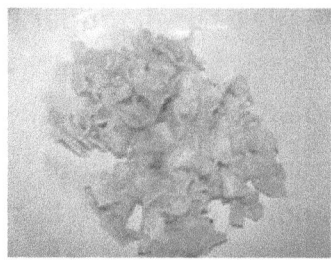

These rich noodles make a great compliment to any meat dish, but you can also eat them with a green salad for a vegetarian meal.

Serves 8 (place into two bags for 2 servings of 4 each).
Method: Make noodles and freeze. Reheat when ready to eat.

Ingredients:
- 16 ounces wide no-egg noodles
- ½ c. grated parmesan cheese
- 1 c. half and half
- 1 package (4 ½ teas.) Good Seasons dry Italian dressing mix
- Salt and pepper to taste
- ¼ c. butter, softened

To prepare for the freezer: Cook the noodles for half the time noted on the bag. Drain and put them in a large bowl. Add butter to bowl and stir to coat the noodles with the butter. Add half and half, the cheese and the dressing mix. Stir well. Cool and place into freezer bags.

When you're ready to eat: Thaw overnight in the refrigerator. Place the bag in the microwave and heat until hot, or put the noodles into a microwave-safe bowl or container and heat.

Mashed Potatoes

Keep these on hand to make quick work of putting fresh mashed potatoes on the dinner at night. Double or triple the recipe so you can put more away in the freezer.

Serves 4.
Method: Prepare fully and heat when ready to eat.

Ingredients:
- 6 russet potatoes, scrubbed
- 4 tab. unsalted butter
- 2-4 tab. milk
- Salt and pepper to taste

To prepare for the freezer: Place potatoes in a medium saucepan and boil until tender and nearly falling apart. Drain. Put potatoes back into pan and place over low heat for about 2 minutes to "dry out" the potatoes and keep them hot. Melt the butter in a small saucepan over low heat and add to the potatoes in the pan. Mix the potatoes until light and fluffy, adding milk and mixing until potatoes are smooth. Add salt and pepper to taste.

Freeze potatoes in a large freezer bag or a foil pan and freeze.

When ready to eat: Thaw overnight in the refrigerator. Place foil pan into a 350-degree oven, or spoon potatoes from bag into a baking pan. Bake until hot all the way through, about 20 minutes, stirring halfway through.

Freezer Cole Slaw

This Cole slaw makes a crispy, crunchy salad that stays crunchy even after a stint in the freezer. Make a double batch so you can always have some of this tasty slaw on hand.

Serves 8 (freeze in two containers to get 2 servings of 4).
Method: Prepare and freeze. Simply thaw when ready to eat.

Ingredients:
- 1 head of cabbage, shredded
- 1 red bell pepper, chopped fine
- 1 red onion, chopped fine
- 1 ¼ c. sugar
- 1 teas. Salt
- 1 c. apple cider vinegar

- ½ c. water

To prepare for the freezer: Mix chopped vegetables. Mix remaining ingredients (sugar, salt, vinegar and water) and place in a saucepan. Bring to a boil and boil for about 3 minutes. Let cool. When cool, pour over vegetables. Freeze this slaw in a hard-sided container.

When you're ready to eat: Thaw overnight in refrigerator. Slaw will be crunchy and crispy when you're ready to eat.

California Pilaf

A great, healthy side dish, this can be prepared in less than 20 minutes right from the freezer.

Serves 6.
Method: Start pilaf, freeze, and finish cooking when ready to eat.

Ingredients:
- 2 c. quick-cooking brown rice
- 1 c. celery, diced small
- ½ c. onion, diced small
- ½ c. dry spaghetti, broken into 1" pieces
- ¼ c. unsalted butter
- 2 teas. chicken bouillon granules
- 1 teas. parsley flakes
- ½ teas. ground thyme
- ¼ teas. ground pepper

To have on serving day:
- 2 c. water

To prepare for the freezer: Sauté the rice, celery, onion and pasta in the butter in a large skillet set over medium heat. Stir constantly until the rice and pasta are golden brown. Stir in the parsley flakes, ground thyme and pepper. Remove from heat and stir in the bouillon granules.

Cool completely and put the mixture into a small freezer bag or a plastic container. Freeze.

When you're ready to eat: Thaw overnight in the refrigerator. Place mixture in a saucepan or skillet with a lid. Add water and heat over medium heat, bringing the mixture to a boil. Once boiling, reduce heat to a simmer. Cover pan and cook for 10 minutes. Remove the pan from the heat and let stand for 10 minutes before serving.

Soups

Soups are some of the most versatile of all freezer dishes. Most soups can be completely made and frozen; just reheat and eat! Soups are not only fast to prepare from the freezer, but are some of the healthiest of all foods you can put in the freezer. It's a great idea to always keep a few frozen soups on hand.

Chicken Noodle Soup

A perennial favorite, you should always have at least one meal of this on hand.

Serves 4.
Method: Cook soup and freeze, adding noodles just before serving.

Ingredients:

- 2 tab. olive oil
- 2 medium carrots, peeled and chopped small
- 1 small onion, chopped fine
- 2 ribs celery, chopped small
- 2 bay leaves
- Salt
- Pepper
- 3 (14 ½ oz.) cans low-sodium chicken broth
- 1 lb. chicken breast tenders, cut into bite-size chunks

To have on serving day:
- 1/2 lb. wide egg noodles

To prepare for the freezer: Put a large pot over medium heat and add olive oil. Add vegetables to the pot in the order they are listed. Add bay leaves and season the vegetables with salt and pepper to state. Add the broth, tenderloins and bring the soup to a boil; reduce heat to medium. Cook the soup for about 5 minutes. Remove from the heat and let cool. Freeze.

When you're ready to eat: Thaw soup overnight in refrigerator. Before serving, pour contents of bag into a large saucepot and bring to a boil. Once boiling, add the egg noodles and cook, stirring frequently, over medium heat until the noodles are cooked, about 5 to 7 minutes. If you like your soup thinner, add water until it's the consistency you like. Taste, season with salt and pepper.

Lentil Soup

Serves 6.
Method: Cook and freeze soup; reheat when ready to eat.

Ingredients:
- 1 small onion, chopped
- ¼ c. olive oil
- 4 carrots, diced
- 2 cloves garlic, minced
- 2 teas. dried oregano
- 2 bay leaves
- 2 teas. dried basil
- 1 (14 ½ oz.) can chopped tomatoes
- 2. c. dry lentils
- 8 c. water

To have on serving day:
- ½ c. baby spinach, rinsed and thinly sliced
- 2 tab. lemon juice
- Salt
- Pepper

To prepare for the freezer: In a large sauce pot, heat the oil over medium heat. Add the onions, carrots and celery. Cook and stir until onion is tender and translucent. Stir in garlic, bay leaves, oregano and basil. Cook for 2 minutes more.

Stir in the lentils and add water and tomatoes. Bring to a boil, then reduce heat and simmer for about 1 hour. Cool and freeze.

When you're ready to serve: Thaw soup overnight in refrigerator. Add contents of freezer bag or container to large saucepot and heat, over medium heat, until hot. Add spinach and lemon juice. Season to taste with salt and pepper. Taste, adjust seasonings and serve.

Creamy Carrot Soup

This soup makes a great side dish, starter or vegetarian entrée.

Serves 6.

Method: Reheat when ready to eat.

Ingredients:
- 2 tab. unsalted butte
- 1 medium onion, finely chopped
- 1 ½ lb. carrots, peeled and slices small (you should have about 5 cups of carrots)
- ½ teas. salt
- Black pepper
- 4 c. chicken broth or stock
- ½ c. part-skim ricotta cheese
- 2 tab. port wine

To have on serving day:
- 2 tab. chopped fresh dill

To prepare for the freezer: Melt butter in a saucepan over medium-low heat and add the onions. Cook until the onions are translucent, about 8 to 10 minutes. Add the carrots, salt, pepper (to taste) and chicken broth. Cook over low heat for about 30 minutes.

Strain the carrots over the saucepan. Puree the solids in a food processor with the ricotta and about 1 cup of the cooking liquid. Conversely, you can use an immersion blender to blend the solids, adding the ricotta right into the pot.

Once it's blended, let soup cool and then freeze.

When you're ready to eat: Let thaw overnight in refrigerator. You can eat this soup hot or cold. To eat cold, simply sprinkle the chopped dill over soup and enjoy. To eat hot, heat it over a low flame until warm. Add dill, stir and serve.

Broccoli-Cheese Soup

Serves 4.

Method: Cook and freeze soup. Reheat when ready to eat.

Ingredients:
- 1 medium onion, chopped fine
- 3 tab. unsalted butter
- ¼ teas. salt
- 1/8 teas. pepper
- 1/8 teas. garlic powder
- 2 c. heavy (whipping) cream
- 1 (14 ½ oz.) can low-sodium chicken broth
- 2 ribs celery, chopped fine
- 1 (10 oz.) frozen broccoli, chopped

To have on serving day:

- 1 ½ c. cheddar cheese, shredded
- ¾ c. mozzarella cheese, shredded
- 6 slices bacon, fried crisp and crumbled
- ¼ c. green onion, chopped
- Shredded cheese for topping

To prepare for the freezer: Sauté onion in butter in a large saucepan until the onion is tender and translucent. Add the garlic powder, salt and pepper. Gradually add the heavy cream and cook over medium heat until bubbly. Meanwhile, in a small saucepan, cook broth, celery and broccoli; once hot cook for about 5 minutes or until the broccoli is tender. Combine both mixtures and cool. When cool, freeze soup.

When you're ready to eat: Heat soup gently over low heat. Stir well; if the soup has separated, use a whisk to make it creamy again. Add cheeses and stir well, cooking until the cheese is melted. Do not let the soup boil. Garnish with bacon bits, green onions and additional shredded cheese if you like.

Minestrone

This is a flavorful soup that freezes well. Double the recipe so you have more to put up in the freezer.

Serves 4.
Method: Make soup and finish off with fresh ingredients when you're ready to serve.

Ingredients:

- 1 tab. olive oil
- 1 clove garlic, minced
- 1 small onion, chopped
- 2 ribs celery, chopped fine
- 2 carrots, diced
- 1 can low-sodium chicken broth
- 1 c. water
- 1 (28 oz.) can diced tomatoes
- 1 (15 oz.) can kidney beans, drained
- 1 cup fresh green beans, trimmed and cut into 1-inch pieces

- 1 teas. dried oregano
- ½ teas. dried basil
- Salt and pepper to taste

To have on serving day:

- 1 c. baby spinach, rinsed
- 1 zucchini, sliced
- ¼ c. small pasta (like seashell)
- Parmesan cheese for topping the soup

To prepare for the freezer: Heat olive oil over medium heat in a large saucepot. Sauté onion and garlic until soft; add celery and carrots and sauté until vegetables are soft. Add rest of ingredients; bring to a boil and reduce heat, simmering for about 30 minutes. Let cool.

Once cool, spoon soup into a large freezer bag or plastic container. Freeze.

When you're ready to eat: Thaw overnight in refrigerator. Pour contents of bag into a large saucepot; add spinach and zucchini and cook, stirring occasionally, for about 15 minutes or until everything is heated through and zucchini is soft.

Meanwhile, cook pasta until al dente. Add pasta into soup and serve.

Vegetable Chowder

Serves 6
Method: Cook soup about halfway through and finish on serving day.

Ingredients:

- 2 tab. unsalted butter
- ½ small onion, chopped fine
- 4 medium carrots, peeled and cut into ½-inch chunks
- ¾ teas. salt
- ½ teas. pepper

To have on serving day:

- 12 oz. red-skinned potatoes, cut into ½-inch pieces
- 2 tab. all-purpose flour
- 1 c. whole milk
- 8 oz. green beans, ends trimmed and cut into 1-inch pieces (or 8 oz. frozen green beans)
- 1 ½ c. frozen corn
- 1 c. frozen peas
- 2 teas. dried thyme

To prepare for the freezer: Melt butter in a 4-quart or larger saucepan set over medium heat. Add onions, carrots, salt and pepper. Cook for about 5 minutes, stirring occasionally, or until the vegetables are soft but not browned. Cool mixture and freeze, making sure to get all the browned bits from the bottom of the pan into the freezer mixture.

When you're ready to eat: Let thaw overnight in refrigerator. Add mixture to a slow cooker and stir well. Add flour and stir well with vegetables. Add 3 cups of water and remaining vegetables. Cook on high for about 2 hours or low for 4 hours, or until vegetables are tender. Add milk and thyme and stir well. Cook for about 10 minutes more.

Sausage And Bean Soup

Serves 4.
Method: Freeze soup and add pasta when ready to eat.

Ingredients:

- 1 teas. olive oil
- 1 lb. pork sausage
- 2 carrots, chopped fine
- 3 stalks celery, chopped fine
- 2 teas. garlic, minced
- 1 teas. dried basil
- 1 teas. dried rosemary
- ½ teas. dried red pepper flakes
- 2 (32 oz.) cartons low-sodium chicken broth
- 2 (14 ½ oz.) cans diced tomatoes with juice
- 2 (15 oz.) cans kidney beans, rinsed and drained
- To have on serving day:
- 8 oz. pasta (macaroni noodles work well)

To prepare for the freezer: Brown sausage in olive oil, breaking up sausage as it cooks and cooking until no longer pink. Add carrots, celery and garlic, cooking until tender. Add rest of ingredients, stirring well. Bring to a boil; lower heat and cook for about 30 minutes, stirring occasionally. Cool and freeze.

When you're ready to eat: Thaw soup overnight in refrigerator. Cook pasta and drain. Reheat soup over medium heat. When hot, add cooked pata and stir until well blended.

Taco Soup

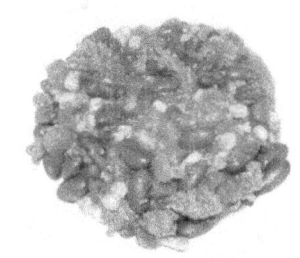

Serves 6 to 8.
Method: Make soup and freeze. Reheat when ready to eat.

Ingredients:

- 1 pound hamburger
- 1 onion, chopped
- 1 ¼ oz. packet taco seasoning
- 1 oz. packet ranch dressing mix
- 2 (15 ¼ oz.) cans kidney beans
- 1 (14 ½ oz.) can diced tomatoes
- 1 (15 oz.) can black beans
- 1 (10 oz.) can tomatoes with chilies (like Ro-Tel)

- 1 (15 ¼ oz.) can corn
- 2 (5 ½ oz. each) cans V-8 juice

To have on serving day:

- Grated cheese
- Tortilla chips
- Sour cream

To prepare for the freezer: Brown hamburger with the onion. When the hamburger is cooked, drain and place in a large saucepot. Add all ingredients and stir, bringing to a boil. Once boiling, cook for about 45 minutes or until an hour.

Spoon the soup into gallon-size freezer bags or into hard-sided plastic containers. You might want to divide this into two meals, or keep it for one meal depending on the size of your family.

When you're ready to eat: Thaw overnight in the refrigerator. Heat on stove top or in microwave. Top with desired additions and enjoy.

Pasta Fagioli Soup

This soup is more stew-like in consistency and it's a rich and comforting dish.

Serves 8.
Method: Cook soup and add pasta right before serving.

Ingredients:

- 1 pound ground beef
- 1 small onion, diced small
- 1 carrot, diced small
- 2 stalks celery, chopped small
- 2 cloves garlic, minced
- 2 (14 ½ oz.) cans diced tomatoes
- 1(15 oz. each) can red kidney beans (do not drain)
- 1 (15 oz.) can great northern beans
- 1 (15 oz.) can tomato sauce
- 1 (12 oz.) can V-8 juice
- 1 tab. white vinegar
- 1 teas. salt
- 1 teas. oregano

- 1 teas. basil
- ½ teas. pepper
- ½ teas. thyme

To have on serving day:
- ½ lb. small pasta (like ditali)

To prepare for the freezer: Brown the ground beef in a large skillet over medium heat. Drain fat and add onions, celery, carrots and garlic. Cook for 10 minutes. Add all remaining ingredients and cook for 45 minutes. Place in a plastic container or freezer bag and freeze until ready to use.

When you're ready to eat: Thaw soup overnight in refrigerator. Place contents of bag into a saucepan and heat over low heat for about 20 to 30 minutes. Meanwhile, cook pasta in a large pot of boiling water. When pasta is al dente, drain and add to soup in pot. Stir until mixed in well.

White Chili

This chili is warming and comforting; you'll want to keep it in the freezer throughout the winter months.

Serves 8.
Method: Cook and freeze. Reheat before serving.

Ingredients:

- 1 lb. ground chicken
- 2 tab. olive oil
- 2 small onions (or 1 large onion), chopped
- 1 (4 oz.) can diced green chilies
- 2 teas. ground cumin
- 1 teas. dried oregano
- 2 c. low-sodium chicken broth
- 2 (14 ½ oz.) cans great Northern beans, rinsed and drained

To have on serving day:
- 1 c. Monterey Jack cheese, shredded

To prepare for the freezer: Cook chicken in a large skillet and set aside.

In a large saucepan, sauté onions and garlic on the olive oil until translucent. Stir in the chilies, cumin and oregano. Stir. Cook for about 2 minutes more. Add the broth, chicken and beans. Add 1 can of water if you want the chili less thick. Reduce heat to a simmer and cook, uncovered for about 15 minutes. Cool, and freeze.

When you're ready to eat: Thaw overnight in refrigerator. Pour chili into a saucepan and heat until hot; if needed, add broth or water to thin. Remove from heat, serve, and add shredded Monterey Jack to each serving.

Sweets

Sweets are some of the easiest things to keep in the freezer. Most favorite dessert and cookie recipes can be converted to freezer cooking. Even a cobbler can be frozen, in components. Freeze the topping separate from the fruit, and then put it together when you're ready to eat. The recipes in this chapter will give you some ideas about how to incorporate more sweets into your freezer cooking sessions.

Strawberry Granita

This is a yummy and cooling dessert for the summer months, and it makes a great end to an elegant meal. Serve in crystal flutes for a special presentation.

Serves 12.
Method: Keep in freezer.

Ingredients:

- ½ c. sugar
- 2 pints strawberries, hulled, chopped
- 1 tablespoon fresh lemon juice

To prepare for the freezer: Heat sugar and 1 cup water in a medium saucepan. Boil over high heat, stirring occasionally. Reduce heat to medium; cook mixture for 1 minute more or until the sugar dissolves completely. Remove the saucepan from the heat to let the sugar syrup cool slightly.

In a food processor with a knife blade attached (or a blender), pulse strawberries until almost smooth. Add the sugar syrup to the strawberries and pulse until just mixed

Pour the strawberry mixture into a 9" x 9" baking pan. Cover with plastic wrap. Freeze until partially frozen, which takes about 2 hours. Stir with a fork. Freeze until completely firm and frozen, about 3 hours or overnight.

When you're ready to eat: Let the granita stand at room temperature for about 10 minutes to soften slightly. Scrape a fork across the surface of the granite to create a pebbly texture. Makes about 6 cups or 12 servings.

Black And White Cheesecake Squares

These are delicious and a great item to put out when entertaining. Wrap these individually and put them out for an after-dinner treat or bring to a party.

Makes 24 pieces.
Method: Make, bake and freeze. Thaw when you are ready to eat.

Ingredients:

- 1 pkg. (12 oz.) semi-sweet chocolate chips
- ½ c. unsalted butter
- 2 c. graham cracker crumbs
- 1 pkg. (8 oz.) cream cheese, softened
- 1 (14 oz.) can sweetened condensed milk
- 1 egg
- 1 teas. vanilla

To prepare for the freezer: Preheat oven to 325. Place the chocolate chips and butter in a medium saucepot over low heat. Heat until chips and butter are melted. Stir until smooth. Stir in the graham cracker crumbs and remove ½ cup of the mixture for later use. Press the remaining graham cracker crumb mixture evenly into an 11" x 9" pan.

In a large bowl, beat the cream cheese with an electric mixer until smooth. Gradually beat in the condensed milk, the egg and vanilla. Pour over the prepared crust. Sprinkle the mixture with the reserved ½ cup crumb mixture. Bake until set, about 30 to 45 minutes. Cool completely.

Once cool, refrigerate until cold (about 2 hours) and then cut into 24 bars. Wrap each bar in saran wrap and place each bar into a large freezer bag.

When you're ready to eat: Thaw these on the countertop until thawed, about an hour or so. Unwrap and enjoy.

Yogurt Popsicles

You can play around with this recipe to create flavor combinations that work for you. You can purchase Popsicle molds at the drug store for as little as $2, or use small paper cups with a popsicle stick frozen inside.

Makes 4.
Method: Freeze and enjoy right out of the freezer.

Ingredients:

- 1c. plain yogurt (try with Greek yogurt for a change)
- 1 banana, sliced
- 1 teas. vanilla
- 1 c. fruit juice (such as orange juice) or fruit chunks (try this with peach chunks)

To prepare for the freezer: Place all ingredients in a blender and blend until smooth. Pour into mold and freeze.

When you're ready to eat: Let popsicles sit for a few minutes or dip into hot water to soften mix.

Chocolate Pudding Cake

This is an impressive and comforting dessert, but it has a few steps that might deter you from making it on a regular basis. Freeze the dry ingredients and include instructions on the bag for how to make this and you'll have this homey and rich dessert on the table in no time.

Serves 6.

Method: Freeze components of recipe, have some fresh ingredients on hand and put this together in under 5 minutes.

Ingredients:

Cake:

- 1 c. flour
- 2 teas. baking powder
- ¼ teas. salt
- Pinch ground cinnamon
- ¾ c. sugar
- 3 tab. unsweetened cocoa powder

Topping:

- ¾ c. sugar

- 3 tab. unsweetened cocoa powder

To have on serving day:

- ¼ c. unsalted butter
- ½ c. milk
- ¾ teas. vanilla

To prepare for the freezer: Place the cake ingredients on one bag with these instructions: "Melt ¼ c. butter and let cool. Pour contents of bag into a large mixing bowl and add the butter, milk and vanilla. Stir well. Spread batter into a 9" x 9" pan."

Place the topping ingredients in another bag with these instructions: "Sprinkle on top of cake before placing in oven." Freeze both bags.

When you're ready to eat: Preheat oven to 350 degrees. When the wet ingredients are mixed, spread into the 9" x 9" pan. Sprinkle the dry mix over and then put 1 ½ c. very hot water over all. Do not stir.

Bake until the top looks crisp and crackled and a knife stuck into the cake part comes out clean, about 30 to 35 minutes. Serve warm with whipped cream or ice cream, if desired.

Ricotta Cheese Cookies

Most cookies can be frozen in various states of baking. These are baked and then glazed after they thaw. For many recipes, you can freeze cookie balls and simply bake when ready to eat. Think how much money you can save if you bake cookies at home rather than buy frozen or refrigerated dough.

Makes about 6 dozen cookies.
Method: Bake and freeze. Thaw, then glaze and add sprinkles before serving.

Ingredients:
- 2 c. sugar

- 1 c. unsalted butter, softened

- 1 (15 oz.) container ricotta cheese

- 2 teas. vanilla

- 2 large eggs

- 4 c. flour

- 2 tab. baking powder

- 1 teas. salt

To have on serving day:
- 1 ½ c. powdered sugar

- 3 tab. milk

- Sprinkles for cookies

To prepare for the freezer: Preheat oven to 350 degrees. Beat sugar and butter in a large bowl with an electric mixer until well blended. Increase mixer speed to high and beat until light and fluffy, about 5 minutes. At medium speed, add in ricotta, vanilla and eggs until well combined.

Reduce the mixer speed to low. Add the flour, baking powder and salt. Beat until a dough forms.

Drop the dough by level tablespoons (or a small cookie scoop size) onto an ungreased cookie sheet, about 2 inches apart. Bake about 15 minutes or until cookies are very lightly golden (cookies will be soft). With a spatula, remove cookies to a wire rack to cool completely.

When cool, place cookies into large freezer bags.

When you're ready to eat: Thaw cookies completely. Sift powdered sugar and then add milk, stirring until a smooth glaze results. Spread icing on cookies and then sprinkle with sugar sprinkles. Set aside to allow icing to dry completely, about 1 hour.

Chocolate Almond Cake

This is a great cake to make at the holidays. It makes two 9" round cakes, so you can make one to enjoy on your cooking day and one to freeze!

Makes two 9" round cakes.
Method: Bake and freeze. Thaw and enjoy.

Ingredients:
- 2 c. all-purpose flour
- 1 teas. baking powder
- 1 teas. baking soda
- ½ teas. salt
- 1 ½ sticks (3/4 c.) unsalted butter, softened
- ¾ c. brown sugar, packed
- ¼ c. honey
- 1 teas. almond extract
- 3 eggs
- ½ c. whole milk
- 1 c. semi-sweet chocolate chips

Streusel:

- ½ c. brown sugar, packed

- ½ c. all-purpose flour
- ¼ c. unsalted butter
- ¾ c. sliced almonds
- ½ c. semi-sweet chocolate chips

Glaze:
- 1 c. chocolate chips
- 1 tab. unsalted butter
- 1 tab. whole milk

To prepare for the freezer: Preheat oven to 350 degrees. Combine flour, baking powder, baking soda and salt in a small bowl. In a large mixing bowl, beat the butter, sugar, honey and almond extract. Add eggs one at a time, beating well after each addition. Gradually beat in the flour mixture, alternating it with the milk.

Stir in 1 cup of the chocolate chips. Divide the batter between two 9-inch round cake pans that have been sprayed with non-stick cooking spray.

Prepare the streusel by stirring the brown sugar and flour together. Cut the butter into the mixture with two forks or a pastry tool. Stir in almonds and chocolate chips. Sprinkle this mixture over the cakes, dividing equally between the two cakes.

Bake the cakes for 25 to 30 minutes or until a toothpick inserted near the center comes out clean. Let cool for 15 minutes.

To prepare the glaze, melt the chocolate chips, butter and milk over low heat until melted and shiny. Stir well. Drizzle this over the cooled cakes. Let cool completely. Wrap well and freeze.

When you're ready to eat: Let the cake thaw on the countertop for about 2 hours or until it reaches room temperature. Slice and enjoy.

Miscellaneous

This chapter gives you a good idea of the sheer variety of foods you can keep on hand in the freezer. From sauces and lunch box goodies, there's limitless potential here.

Chewy Granola Bars

These are a great addition to a lunchbox. Simply freeze and pull out when making lunches. They will be thawed and ready to eat by lunchtime.

Makes about 18 serving
Ingredients:

- 1 cup brown sugar
- ¼ cup white sugar
- ½ cup butter (1 stick), softened
- 2 tab. honey
- 1 teas. vanilla
- 1 egg
- 1 c. flour
- 1 ½ teas. cinnamon
- ½ teas. baking powder
- ¼ teas. salt
- 1 ¼ c. rolled oats
- 1 ¼ c. crispy rice cereal (like Rice Krispies)
- 1 c. chocolate chips
- ½ c. slivered almonds, optional

To prepare for the freezer: Combine sugars and butter in bowl and cream with a mixer until fluffy. Add the honey, vanilla and egg. Mix well. Blend in the dry ingredients – the flour, cinnamon, baking soda and salt. Stir in the remaining ingredients by hand. Press firmly into the bottom of a greased 13" x 9" pan.

Bake at 350 degrees for 18 to 20 minutes or until set. Bars will firm as they coll. Once it cools, cut into bars. Wrap each bar in plastic wrap and place all bars into a large freezer bag.

When you're ready to eat: Pull out desired number of granola bars and pack in lunch bag. These will be thawed by lunch. Or thaw on kitchen counter. These can also be thawed in a microwave for 20 seconds or until thawed or serve warm.

Chicken Broth

Keep chicken broth on hand for homemade soups, for adding to pasta dishes and for other cooking needs. The chicken broth you make will be much lower in sodium than store-bought broth. Whenever you have a chicken carcass on hand (either from a homemade chicken or a rotisserie you buy at the grocery store), take time to make chicken broth.

Makes varied amount depending on your ingredients and how much water you use.
Method: Make broth and freeze for future use. Use as is, adding to recipes as needed.

Ingredients:
- 1 chicken carcass, meat removed
- 3 carrots
- 3 stalks of celery (no need to trim)
- ½ small onion, quartered
- Salt
- Pepper
- Seasonings as desired (sage, rosemary or garlic powder)

To prepare for the freezer: Place all ingredients into a large stock pot. Add water to cover. Bring to a boil and boil for about 10 minutes, then reduce heat and cook for another 30 minutes or so. Remove carcass and vegetable solids from water carefully with tongs. Cover pot and put in the refrigerator overnight.

The next day, remove the pot from the refrigerator, skim the fat solids from the top of the broth and prepare broth for freezing. You can freeze this in ice cube trays (for when you only need a little chicken broth) or you can freeze it in 1-cup amounts.

When you're ready to use: Thaw overnight in refrigerator and use as needed. If you have frozen the broth in ice cube trays, you can add the small cubes to a soup or other boiling liquid.

Bean And Cheese Burritos

Sure, you can buy these pre-made and they are very inexpensive, but they are also filled with a lot of junk. It's so easy to make them yourself; simply heat and eat.

Makes 12.
Method: Make burritos, freeze, and heat when needed.

Ingredients:
- Refried beans (about 3 smaller cans)
- 12 flour tortillas
- 6 oz. cheddar cheese, shredded
- ½ c. salsa

To prepare for the freezer: Warm tortillas in microwave or oven until pliable. On each tortilla, place down the middle a large spoonful (or about ¼ cup) refried beans, shredded cheddar cheese and a small amount of salsa. Fold like a burrito, making sure to tuck in the ends, and wrap in waxed paper. Place burritos in freezer bag and freeze.

When you're ready to eat: To microwave, place in microwave for 2 minutes, turn over and microwave 1 to 2 minutes longer or until hot throughout. To heat in the oven, preheat oven to 350 and bake for 20 to 30 minutes or until heated throughout.

Stuffed Shells

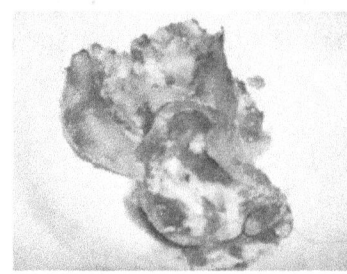

This is a great vegetarian dish that even die-hard meat eaters will enjoy. It's tasty, filling and healthy.

Serves 6 with leftovers; if you want smaller portions, divide into 2 foil pans. You can also easily double or triple this recipe.

Method: Prepare shells and freeze to bake on serving day.

Ingredients:
- 12 ounce box of jumbo shells
- 16 ounces ricotta cheese
- 16 ounces cottage cheese
- 16 ounces mozzarella cheese, shredded
- ½ to ¾ cup parmesan cheese, grated
- 3 eggs

- ¾ teas. oregano

- ½ teas. pepper

To have on serving day:
Spaghetti sauce, about 1 regular-sized jar or about 3-4 cups of homemade

To prepare for the freezer: Cook the shells until limp, but not fully cooked. Drain them and cool them in a single layer on waxed paper. While they are cooling, prepare filling. Combine all the cheeses, the eggs, oregano and pepper. Add ½ teaspoon of salt if you like. Fill each shell with about 1 ½ to 2 tablespoons of the cheese mixture. Place these in a single layer in 9" x 9" foil pan. If you are using homemade sauce, freezer the right amount in a freezer bag and store with the shells in the freezer.

When you're ready to eat: Thaw the shells (and sauce, if using homemade). Spread about ½ cup to 1 cup of spaghetti sauce on the bottom of the foil pan, working it around the shells. Pour the remaining sauce over the shells and bake at 350 for about 25 to 30 minutes or until the shells are hot throughout.

Healthy Pancake Syrup

You can make this and freeze in small plastic containers or in an ice cube tray. Thaw on low in the microwave and you have healthy, homemade pancake, waffle or French toast syrup whenever you need it.

Makes 6 cups.
Method: Make and freeze; thaw desired amount and use as needed.

Ingredients:
- ¼ c. cornstarch
- 4 c. cold water
- 2 (12 oz.) cans frozen apple juice concentrate
- ¼ c. sugar
- 1 teas. maple extract

To prepare for the freezer: Mix the cornstarch in 1 cup of water until dissolved. In a large saucepan over medium heat, combine the juice, remaining water and the water/cornstarch solution. Cook, stirring from frequently to constantly, for about 4 minutes. Add the sugar. Continue cooking until the mixture thickens (10 to 15 minutes). Once the mixture is as thick as syrup and clear, add the maple extract. Let cool completely.

Freeze in ice cube trays or small freezer bags or plastic storage containers.

When you're ready to eat: Remove desired amount from the freezer and heat in the microwave until thawed, about 2 to 5 minutes depending on the amount.

Note: You can also use the warm syrup over desserts, like ice cream, cheesecake or lava cake.

Freezing Fruit

You can freeze fruit at the peak of freshness and save money on frozen fruit. And because you froze it, you control ingredients and even where the fruit came from. Pick your own fruit and freeze it and have organic fruit throughout the year.

The fruits that are best for freezing include:

- Strawberries
- Raspberries
- Blackberries
- Peaches
- Blueberries
- Pineapple

To freeze fruit, follow these steps:
1 Clean fruit and let try well.

2 If using berries, hull them; if freezing peaches, remove pit.

3 If using peaches or pineapple, cut into bite-size pieces.

4 Place fruit on a parchment-lined or waxed paper-lined baking sheet so pieces are not touching.

5 Place the baking sheet in the freezer and freeze until solid, about 1 hour.

6 Once solid, place the fruit into a freezer bag.

7 Fruit keeps well for at least 6 months.

Busy Bananas

These banana bites for the freezer are called "busy" because they have a lot going on, even though there are only 4 ingredients. These are great for lunch boxes (put them in the lunch box when frozen and they'll thaw before lunch) or for snacking on right out of the freezer. They are a great source of energy and the nutrients from the banana.

Makes 10 to 12 banana pieces.
Method: Make and keep in the freezer for snacking.

Ingredients:
- 2 large bananas
- ¼ to ½ c. chocolate chips
- ¼ c. peanut butter
- ¼ to 1/2 c. shredded coconut

To prepare for the freezer: Place a piece of waxed paper or parchment paper on a cookie sheet. Set aside.

Slice bananas into chunks. You'll get around 5 to 6 pieces from each large banana. Heat the peanut butter and chocolate chips in the microwave until melted, about 1 minute. Stir until smooth.

Carefully dip the banana pieces into the chocolate/peanut butter mixture, covering just one end of the banana chunk. Then dip into the coconut. Place on the prepared cookie sheet.

Put cookie sheet in freezer and freeze until solid. When frozen, put the banana bites into a freezer container.

When you're ready to eat: Just remove from the freezer and eat from frozen.

Peanut Butter And Jelly Sandwiches

If the morning lunch-making rush has you down, make sandwiches ahead of time. You can make meat sandwiches ahead of time, but the quality will be affected (though you can very successfully freeze lunch meat in small packages, perfect for pulling out the night before for fresh sandwiches). If you learn a few quick tricks, however, you can make perfect peanut butter and jelly sandwiches for the freezer; pull them out when making lunches and they'll be thawed perfectly in time for lunch.

If you're familiar with Uncrustables, these are quite similar to those.

Makes 10 sandwiches.

Method: Freeze pre-made sandwiches and thaw when ready to eat.

Ingredients:

- 20 slices bread (white works best with a sandwich sealer, but wheat will work as well)

- Peanut butter

- Jelly (any flavor works, the thicker the better)

- Sandwich sealer (this is a tool you can buy in the grocery store or online that will simultaneously seal the sandwich and remove the crusts as well.

To prepare for the freezer: For each sandwich, spread peanut butter on both sides of the bread and put jelly on one piece of bread. Put the two pieces together. The peanut butter provides a sort of barrier so the sandwich can freeze without the jelly causing the bread to get mushy. Use the sandwich sealer to seal the sides. You can also just place these in the freezer without using a sealer. Wrap in freezer paper or wax paper before freezing.

When you're ready to eat: These will thaw in about 30 to 45 minutes, so you can pull them out before preparing your meal, or pull them out in the morning and pack them in lunchboxes for eating once the kids are ready for lunch.

Homemade "Refried" Beans

These aren't truly refried because you don't fry them, but they are mashed and flavored like refried beans and you can use them anywhere you might use refried beans. They are much better for you, can be more flavorful and are much less expensive.

Makes 8 servings.
Method: Make beans, partially mash and freeze. Reheat when ready to eat.

Ingredients:
- 1 pound dried pinto beans
- 1 small onion, chopped fine
- Salt
- Pepper
- Garlic powder
- Cumin (optional)

To prepare for the freezer: Start the day before you will make these. Place beans in a colander and rinse, while picking out the beans that are defective or rocks that you find in the mix. Once rinsed, place it into a bowl and cover with water. Leave overnight.

The next day, drain the water and put the beans in a slow cooker. Add onion and cover with enough water so it's about an inch more than beans. Cook on low for 8 to 10 hours or until beans are tender. Add salt and pepper to taste. Mash beans with a handheld potato masher until beans are the consistency you like. Season with salt and pepper to taste, add garlic powder to taste and add cumin to taste if you want it.

Package these in small plastic freezer containers or small freezer bags; freeze them in portions appropriate for your family.

When you're ready to eat: Thaw overnight in refrigerator. Heat on stovetop or in microwave and enjoy.

Slow Cooker Spaghetti Sauce

Have this cooking away during your cooking day and then freeze in meal-sized portions. If you like, you can add browned hamburger or sausage to the sauce before you use it, or keep it vegetarian. Use this as a pasta sauce, pizza sauce, dip for pizza rolls or calzone or as a base for an Italian soup.

Makes about 16 servings.
Method: Cook sauce in slow cooker and freeze in meal-sized portions.

Ingredients:
- 2 medium onions, chopped fine
- 2 (28 oz. each) cans diced tomatoes, undrained
- 1 (16 oz.) can tomato sauce
- 2 (8 oz.) cans tomato paste
- 2 bay leaves
- 2 tab. brown sugar
- 6 cloves garlic, minced
- 2-3 teas. dried basil
- 2-3 teas. dried oregano
- 2 teas. salt
- 1 ½ teas. dried thyme

To prepare for the freezer: Add all ingredients to a slow cooker and cover. Cook on low for 7-8 hours or until heated through and flavors are well melded. Discard bay leaf. Place into freezer bags or plastic containers and freeze.

When you're ready to eat: Thaw overnight in refrigerator or heat slowly in a microwave until thawed and heated through. Use as you like.

www.ingramcontent.com/pod-product-compliance
Lightning Source LLC
Chambersburg PA
CBHW071440070526
44578CB00001B/156